The
Total TxtMSg
Dictionary

compiled
and edited by
Andrew John
with **Stephen Blake**

Michael O'Mara Books Limited

First published in Great Britain in 2001 by
Michael O'Mara Books Limited
9 Lion Yard, Tremadoc Road
London SW4 7NQ

Devised by Gabrielle Mander

A CIP catalogue record for this book is available
from the British Library

ISBN 1-85479-893-6

1 3 5 7 9 10 8 6 4 2

Designed and typeset by Martin Bristow

Printed and bound in Great Britain by Cox & Wyman,
Reading, Berks.

CONTENTS

INTRODUCTION

Shorter ways of saying things have been with us since speech began. 'Ug!' probably carried a multitude of meanings to a Neanderthal – and even today we hear it used by other people's kids.

It is argued that, because we live in a faster age, we need a faster language. The fastest way of communicating, of course, is the telephone, because speech is quick, but here we're concerned with the written and printed word, and that has become shorter with every change in communication.

Until recently, we found abbreviations mainly in specialized worlds such as science (EMR, for instance), the military (Sgt, Lt) and government (DfEE, MAFF). Many international organizations are known by their abbreviations (NATO, UNESCO), as are many charities (RSPCA, Oxfam, RSPB).

We also see the common abbreviations that we've used for years, such as RSVP at the bottom of an invitation and ways of saving money in contact ads by making four words into one when you want to describe an aspect of yourself (GSOH). Then there are the little expressions of affection that were (maybe still are) to be found written on the back of the envelope containing a love letter: SWALK, for instance, or HOLLAND. And of course we have all taken down notes while talking to someone on the telephone and written 'hd' for 'had', 'shd', for 'should', 'btw' for 'between' and so on.

Other abbreviations and acronyms have sprung up from social science, the media and everyday conversation. We don't think twice before speaking of a yuppie or a nimby these days, and often we find they're expressed entirely in lowercase letters, having earned their place in the popular lexicon.

Even in speech we use abbreviations without thinking about it. When we say 'Howdy?' we're saying 'How do you do?' Did 'Hi' come from 'Hiya', and that from 'How are you?'? Who knows? The ubiquitous 'gonna' is on everyone's lips, and, as a shortening of 'going to', is acceptable even in semiformal speech. And then there are the dozens of contractions such as 'we'd' for 'we would' or 'we had', and 'shouldn't' for 'should not'. These are not restricted to speech, of course, and are to be found in all but the most formal writing.

Some abbreviations, as we have seen, are acronyms. An acronym, strictly speaking, must spell a speakable word with its initials. DfEE doesn't count, but NATO does. While Oxfam isn't a set of initials as such, we can just about call it an acronym because elements of its full title, Oxford Committee for Famine Relief, are taken to form a sayable word.

So far, so good. We had a manageable language with many of its words conveniently shortened so that we could communicate more quickly. We all felt comfortable with that. Then came the revolution: email, WAP (look it up) and text messages. Suddenly we find there's an abbreviation for just about anything – not to mention emoticons, but more on those later. Who would have thought – back in those balmy days of having just enough abbreviations to see you through an average day – that you would be able to say, lovingly, to the object of your desire, '**GtOutaMyDrms&In2MyLfe**'? Or that, given a little more familiarity with the desired object, you would be saying, '**HABABWan2GtLckE?**'?

People are doing it all the time.

The beauty of the text message is that it's cheaper than a phone call and it makes it impossible to waffle: because you just don't have the space. What is even better is the way in which ingenious abbreviations have been contrived by text-messagers all over the world to capture a vaguely philosophical thought, a loving sentiment or a beautifully crafted obscenity. Text-messaging is nothing short of a phenomenon, and millions of them per day are crossing streets and crossing continents, some of them merely saying we'll meet up at seven o'clock, others exchanging important business information.

Certain conventions have established themselves as this way of sending brief messages via computer and mobile phone has evolved. You find in many abbreviations that a capital letter will represent a longer vowel sound, while the lowercase letter would represent a shorter one. A capital can also stand in place of a double letter. '**LOks**' represents 'looks', for instance, in '**TOnlyThngThtLOksGOdOnMeIsU**', just as '**GOd**' reads 'good'. Not all are as complicated.

Emoticons (that's in the dictionary, too) are another matter altogether. With these cheeky, almost cryptogrammatical ciphers all sorts of messages are conveyed. They might look oddly at you down at the chippy if you presented them with a note saying you wanted >-> <)))">&{{{{{{ but you could tell your mate on his WAP phone that this is what you're eating at the moment. So you needn't feel a <:-(or even have cause to say <=\ if someone sends you a string of characters from a computer keyboard. You should find the solution in our special section on emoticons. If not, it's because a new one's been invented since I wrote this. And that's why I won't try to say how many million text messages (whether as abbreviations or emoticons, or a mixture of the two) are sent daily, because the last time I looked it was tens of millions. It seems to be rising exponentially.

So, as you browse through this comprehensive dictionary of text-messaging abbreviations, acronyms and emoticons, you'll be fascinated, titillated, educated and occasionally bewildered. What you won't be is bored. In fact, it's **UTU**, but, if you're **U4IT** you'll be **UAN** and will have **TTOYaL**.

Where this dictionary is especially useful is having a dazzling mixture of conventional abbreviations and those that are becoming commonplace on the small screens of mobile phones. Where else would you find, within a few lines of each other, **XML** (extensible markup language) and **XMeQk** (kiss me quick), or **WAAC** (Women's Auxiliary Army Corps) so close to **WALOOR** (what a load of old rubbish)?

This, as well as being mildly amusing, is deliberate. You may be text-messaging a friend with stuff and nonsense one minute, and the next minute get a message from a colleague who's referring to a couple of acts of Parliament, the odd inter-governmental organization and a chemical formula, throwing in an army rank or two for good measure. So it makes sense for you to go out now and buy a dozen more copies of *The Total Txtmsg Dictionary* and give them to your friends, so they'll know what you're talking about!

Who knows? **ATEOTD** (or even **@TEOTD**), writing like this may one day take over completely. (Pitman's shorthand, **EtYa<30ut**.) Then we'll have to bring out a dictionary for people who like to use long words.

I could not have compiled this collection without the indefatigable help of Stephen Blake, who has taken on much of the donkey work and has sought out some of the more obscure and amusing examples.

As far as we've both been able to tell (and they're being invented all the time), the abbreviations in this dictionary are all **U2TM**, so, after studying them for a while, no one can say of you, '**YaLiftDsntREchTTopFlOr**'.

Andrew John
West Wales, February 2001

11

SYMBOLS AND FIGURES

#10	Number Ten Downing Street
%ge	percentage
&AT	and all that
&ILuvUSo	and I love you so
@ATOTDON	at all times of the day or night
@S1EX	at someone else's expense
@TEOTD	at the end of the day
0CnStpUNow	nothing can stop you now
0LeSThnBrL	nothing less than brilliant
0V0G	nothing ventured, nothing gained
1/2msre	half measure
1@AT	one at a time
1A=	first among equals
1C	first class
1DA@ATIm	one day at a time
1LOD	first line of defence
1nc	once
1OTD	one of these days
1sNevaE	one's never enough
1st2K	first to know
1stly	firstly
1StpAwA	one step away
1StpClOsa	one step closer
1sty	firsty (thirsty)

1Wld	First World
1WW	First World War
1C1S	first come, first served
2	to, too, two
2B	to be
2BA	to be announced
2BC	to be continued/confirmed
2BON2BTITQ	to be or not to be, that is the question
2BR	to be resolved
2C	second class
2dAsYaLkEDA	today's your lucky day
2dA	today
2Fw	too few
2Fw2L8	too few, too late
2G2TA	too good to throw away
2G2W	too good to waste
2gtha4Eva	together for ever
2gtha4Eva&Eva	
	together forever and ever
2gthaWeRButiful	
	together we are beautiful
2Hot2Hndl	too hot to handle
2L8	too late
2Lte	too late
2Mch	too much
2MCSTB	too many cooks spoil the broth
2Mny	too many

2moro	tomorrow
2nIte	tonight
2oftn	too often
2SOn	too soon
2SW	to start with
2tyST	twentysomething
2tySTs	twentysomethings
2wcr	twicer
2WW	Second World War
2ErlE	too early
2Mch2Ltle2L8	too much, too little, too late
2WUA*	to wish upon a star
3C	third class
3dom	freedom
3LA	three-letter acronym
3sm	threesome
3sum	threesome
3tyST	thirtysomething
3tySTs	thirtysomethings
3Wld	third world
24/7	twenty-four hours a day, seven days a week
4	for, four
4AM	for a moment/minute
4BOW	for better or worse
4BOW	for better or worse
4ce	force
4COL	for crying out loud

4COL	for crying out loud
4fit	forfeit
4GOd	for good
4grnd	foreground
4GS	for goodness'/God's sake
4gt	forget/forgot
4gtIt	forget it
4gtn	forgotten
4LA	four-letter acronym
4LW	four-letter word
4m	form
4NK8	fornicate
4NK8r	fornicator
4play	foreplay
4ST	for some time
4sum	foursome
4t	fort, fought
4TGr8rGOd	for the greater good
4tnIt	fortnight
4tune	fortune
4tyST	fortysomething
4tySTs	fortysomethings
4WD	four-wheel-drive
4x4	four-by-four (vehicle)
4eva	forever/for ever
4eva+2	forever and ever
4evaInLuv	forever in love

4evaKndOfLuv	forever kind of love
4EvaURS	forever yours
4EvaYRS	forever yours
5tyST	fiftysomething
5tySTs	fiftysomethings
6tyST	sixtysomething
6tySTs	sixtysomethings
7tyST	seventysomething
7tySTs	seventysomethings
8	Ate
8tyST	eightysomething
8tySTs	eightysomethings
8–L8	eight till late
9tyST	ninetysomething
9tySTs	ninetysomethings
9!	no, no way
10Q	thank you
10X	thanks
12?	(do you) want to?
12M	one too many
100HST	onehundredsomething
100HSTs	onehundredsomethings
100ST	onehundredsomething
100STs	onehundredsomethings
102T12	ten to the dozen
102T12	ten to the dozen

A

A ampere
Å angstrom
A2A aim(ing) to avoid
A2EIn2 able to enter into
AA Advertising Association; Alcoholics Anonymous; anti-aircraft; Architectural Association; Associate in Arts; Automobile Association; auto answer
A&A acronyms and abbreviations; again and again
A@A aimed at avoiding
AAA screaming; Amateur Athletics Association; American Automobile Association
AAAIC as able as I can
AAB all-to-all broadcast
AABA ambient air-breathing apparatus; Association of American Business Advisors
AABB American Association of Blood Banks
AABGA American Association of Botanical Gardens and Arboreta
AABP American Association of Bovine Practitioners

AAby as amended by
A@AC avoid(ing) at all costs
AACB Australian Association of Clinical Biochemists
AACR Anglo-American Cataloguing Rules
AACR2 Anglo-American Cataloguing Rules 2nd. ed.
AACSB American Assembly of Collegiate Schools of Business
AAF avoid a Florida (as in US election)
AAGPBL All American Girls' Professional Baseball League
AAM air-to-air missile; as a matter of fact
AAMOF as a matter of fact
AAO all aspects of
AAR against all risks
AASRSOS approved all-employee savings-related share option scheme
AAT and all that; average access time
AATR always at the ready
AATY after all these years
AAUF Association of Advisers for Under Fives
AB able-bodied seaman; *Artium Baccalaureus* (Bachelor of Arts, US); ah bless!; ample bosom
A&B above and beyond
ABA Amateur Boxing Association; American Bar Association; American Basketball Association

ABACUS Association of Bibliographic Agencies of Britain, Australia, Canada and the United States; Association of British, Australian, Canadian and US (National Libraries)

ABAG Association of Bay Area Governments

ABARE Australian Bureau of Agricultural and Resource Economics

ABATS Automatic Bit Access Test System

ABB ASEA Brown Boveri (Swiss-Swedish Technology Company)

Abbr abbreviated

Abbrv abbreviated

ABC Activity Based Costing; Activity-Based Costing; American Broadcasting Company; American Broadcasting Corporation

ABC Alliance of Business Consultants; alphabet; American Broadcasting Corporation; Audit Bureau Circulation; Australian Broadcasting Corporation

ABCA America Britain Canada Australia

ABCC Association of British Chambers of Commerce

ABCCC AirBorne Command Control Communication; Airborne Battlefield Command and Control Center; Airborne Command and Control Center

ABCD Advanced Beam-Weapon Concept Definition; Atomic, Biological, Chemical, Data (warfare)

ABE Association of Business Executives

ABEL Advanced Boolean Expression Language

AbFab absolutely fabulous; *Absolutely Fabulous*

ABH actual bodily harm

ABHI Association of British Healthcare Industries

ABI Association of British Insurers

ABIOS advanced BIOS

ABIST automatic built-in self-test (IBM)

ABLAC Anglican Belgium-Luxembourg Area Council

ABLE adaptive battery life extender

ABM antiballistic missile; asynchronous balanced mode

ABMRC Association of British Market Research Companies

ABP American Business Products

ABPCO Association of British Professional Conference Organizers

ABPR American Book Publishing Record (from *Publishers' Weekly*)

abr abridge

ABR automatic bit band rate detection; available bit rate

Abrd abridged

ABRS Automated Book Request System (British Library)

Abs absent, absence

ABS Acrylonitrile Butadiene-Styrene (plastic); AlkylBenzeneSulphonate (surfactant); Alternative Billing Service; American Bureau of Shipping; Antilock Braking System; Association of Business Schools

ABSA Association of Building Services Agencies; Association for Business Sponsorship of the Arts

ABSBH Average Busy Season Busy Hour

AbsFab! fabulous abdominals!

Absl absolute

Absly absolutely

AbsntMndd absentminded

ABSOLOM Agreement By Sending Out Lots Of Memos

ABSSA African/Black Student Statewide Alliance (A/BSSA)

Abstr abstract

ABT abort

Abt about

Abt2 about to

ABTA Allied Brewery Trades Association; Association of British Travel Agents

A&BTCOD above and beyond the call of duty

ABTT Association of British Theatre Technicians

AbtTrn about turn

Abv above

ABWR Advanced Boiling Water Reactor
AC alternating current
a/c account
A/c2 account to
A/c4 account for
ACA a cut above; Association of Consulting Actuaries
ACABQ Advisory Committee on Administrative and Budgetary Questions
AC/a.c. alternating current
ACAS Advisory, Conciliation and Arbitration Service
ACATR a cut above the rest
ACB American Council of the Blind
ACBL American Contract Bridge League
ACCA Association of Certified Corporate Accountants
ACCENT Association of Centres of Excellence in Foreign Language Training
A/c account
ACD automatic call distribution
ACE access control encryption/entry; Adobe Certified Expert
ACENVO Association of Chief Executives of National Voluntary Organizations
ACF Advisory Committee on Foodstuffs (EU)

ACITT Advisory Committee for Innovation and
Technology Transfer (EU)

Ack acknowledge

Ack-Ack anti-aircraft (AA, from phonetic 'ack' for 'A')

ACL American Consultants League

ACLU American Civil Liberties Union

ACNtu8T+ accentuate the positive

ACO all clapped out

ACOfWelthNowSuRoundsUUDrawFrmThsCALUNEd
a sea of wealth now surrounds you you draw
from this sea all you need

ACOMI a case of mistaken identity

ACP African, Caribbean and Pacific States

ACPO Association of Chief Police Officers

ACS Association of Consulting Scientists

ACSHHPW Advisory Committee on Safety, Hygiene and
Health Protection At Work (EU)

ACST Association of Consulting Science and
Technology

ACT Association of Corporate Treasurers;
Australian Capital Territory

ACTH adrenocorticotropin; Australian Council of
Trade Unions

ACTT Advanced Communication and Timekeeping
Technology (Seiko)

ActYaAgeNtYaShuSIz
act your age, not your shoe size

ACU automatic calling unit
ACV Advisory Committee on Banking (EU)
AD accidental(ly) damage(d); Anno Domini
A–D analogue-to-digital
ADA Automatic Data Acquisitions (Programming Language named after Augusta Ada Lovelace)
ADABAS Adaptable Database System
ADAM Advanced Architecture in Medicine. (EU)
ADC adaptive data compression (protocol) (Hayes); add with carry; aide-de-camp; analog to digital converter
ADCert a dead cert (certainty)
ADctd2Luv addicted to love
ADD Automatic Document Detection (WordPerfect)
Addn addition
Addnl additional(ly)
ADF automatic document feeder; automatically defined function
Adj adjacent
Adj2 adjacent to
ADKMS Advanced Data and Knowledge Management Systems (EU)
Adm administration; Admiralty
ADN any day now
ADO active data objects

ADP adenosine diphosphate; Agricultural Development Programme (EU); automatic data processing

ADQ a direct question . . .

ADR address (computers); alternate dispute resolution

Adrd&Xplrd adored and explored

ADRG Alternative Disputes Resolution Group

AdrnlnRsh adrenalin rush

ADSET Association for Database Services

ADSOS approved discretionary share option scheme

ADST approved deferred share trust

ADT Atlantic Daylight Time

ADU automatic dialling unit

AE above or equal; actively encourage(d)/engage(d)

A&E accident and emergency (casualty department in a hospital)

AEA Atomic Energy Authority (UK)

AEAABC as easy as ABC

AEB analog expansion bus

AEC Agriculture Executive Council; Atomic Energy Commission (USA)

AEE Association for Experiential Education

AEEU Amalgamated Engineering and Electrical Union

AEMI	Advanced Environment for Medical Image Interpretation (EU)
AEMRI	Association of European Market Research Institutes
AEO	Association of Exhibition Organizers
AEP	Association of Educational Psychologists
AESC	Association of Executive Search Consultants
AETT	Association of Educational and Training Technology
AF	*Archers* fanatic; audio frequency
AFA	Association of Flight Attendants
AFAIA	as far as I'm aware
AFAIC	as far as I'm concerned
AFAICC	as far as I can see
AFAICS	as far as I can see
AFAIK	as far as I know/I'm concerned
AFAIP	as far as is possible
AFAIUI	as far as I understand/understood it
AFAP	as far as possible
AFB	air force base
AFBD	Association of Futures Brokers and Dealers
AFBPS	Associate Fellow of the British Psychological Society
AFC	Air Force Cross; American Football Conference; Association of Fundraising Consultants; average fixed cost
AFctnt	affectionate

AFctntlE affectionately

AfDB African Development Bank

AFEmAl alpha female

AFK away from keyboard

AFL/CIO American Federation of Labor/Congress of Industrial Organizations

AFM Air Force Medal; Association of Facilities Managers

AFTP anonymous file transfer protocol

Aftr after

AftrnOn afternoon

AFUNW2G all fucked up, nowhere to go

AFV armoured fighting vehicle

AGA advanced graphics adapter

AGCAS Association of Graduate Careers Advisory Services

AGEFT Agricultural Electronic Fund Transfer (EU)

AGM annual general meeting

AGoNaBmpNoMorW/NoBgFatWmn
ain't gonna bump no more with no big fat woman

AGR advanced gas-cooled reactor

AgrEmnt agreement

AGREP Agricultural Research Projects (EU)

AGREX Agricultural Guarantee Fund Expenditure (EU)

Agt agent

AGT	all good things
AGTWHBA	a good time was had by all
AGW	actual gross weight
AHAP	as humanly as possible
AhB!	Ahhh, Bisto!
AHC	Accepting Houses Committee
Ahd	ahead
AHOEC	Association of Heads of Outdoor Education Centres
AHzBEn	a has-been
AI	analog input; artificial intelligence
AI!	as if . . . !
AIAGDW	all in a good day's work
AIAS	as I've always said
AIChE	American Institute of Chemical Engineers
AICI	as I see it
AICS	Association of Independent Computer Specialists
AID	artificial insemination by donor
AIDA	Advanced Integrated-Circuit Design Aids (EU)
AIDMED	Assistant for Interacting with Multimedia Medical Databases (EU)
AIDS	Acquired Immune Deficiency Syndrome
AIF	Australian Imperial Force
AIFF	Audio Interchange File Format
AIH	artificial insemination by husband

AIM Alternative Investment Market; AOL Instant Messenger

AINFOT all in the fullness of time

Aint0LkeIt ain't nothing like it

Aint0LkeTRThngBAB
ain't nothing like the real thing, baby

AintNoMntnHiEnuf2KEpMeFrmU
ain't no mountain high enough to keep me from you

AintNoStPinUNow
ain't no stopping you now

AIRC Association of Independent Radio Contractors

AIRTO Association of Independent Research and Technology Organizations

AISB as I said before

AISP Association of Information Systems Professionals

AIT Advanced Intelligent Tape (drive) (Sony)

AITC Association of Investment Trust Companies

AITM all in the mind

AITT Association of Industrial Truck Trainers

AIW as it were/was

AIX Advanced Interactive Executive (IBM)

AJA all joking apart

AjAint0BtANo age ain't nothing but a number

AJU all jacked up

AK	Alaska (official postal abbreviation)
AKA	also known as
AL	Alabama (official postal abbreviation); all
AL2gtha	altogether
Alc	alcohol(ic)
ALCM	air-launched cruise missile
ALE	address latch enable; application linking and embedding
ALGOL	algorithmic oriented language
AGTCTAE	all good things come to an end
AGTMCTAE	all good things must come to an end
ALGUS	Alliance and Leicester Group Union of Staff
ALIHve2DoIsDrm	
	all I have to do is dream
ALIkUMEnIt	act like you mean it
Aliph	aliphatic
ALIWanIsU	all I want is you
Alk	alkaline
Alky	alkalinity
ALLIADT	a little learning is a dangerous thing
ALMth&Trsrs	all mouth and trousers
ALNItLng	all night long
ALOrO	all or nothing
ALOvaNow	all over now
ALP	Australian Labor Party
ALP$&Wnd	all piss and wind
ALrIt	all right/alright

Alt alternate; alteration

ALTENER Alternative Energy (initiative on the development of new and renewable energy) (EU)

ALThosCrvs&MeWivNoBrks
all those curves and me with no brakes

ALTImHI all time high

ALtleLuv? a little love?

ALTLuvInTWrld al the love in the world

ALU arithmetic and logic unit

AlwAsLOkOnTBrItSIdOfLIf
always look on the bright side of life

Alwys always

Alwys&4eva always and for ever

AM Albert Medal; Air Ministry; amplitude modulation; *Artium Magister* (Master of Arts, US); Assembly Member

a.m. ante meridiem (before noon)

AM4I! always mad for it

AMA against medical advice

AMAl alpha male

AMAP as much/many as possible

AMBA Association of Masters in Business Administration

AME a moving experience

AMED Association of Management Education and Development

AMEI	Association of Medical Expenses Insurers
AmEx	American Express
AMIS	Agricultural Markets Intelligence System (EU)
AML	all my love
AMLUV	all my love
AMOmntOnTLpsIsALIfTImOnTHips	
	a moment on the lips is a lifetime on the hips
AMSO	Association of Market Survey Organizations
Amt	amount
AMU	atomic mass unit
AN	above named; in the year . . .
ANA	Agricultural Numerical Annexes (EU)
Anal	analysis, analytical(ly)
ANBACIS	Automated Nuclear, Biological, and Chemical Info. System
ANC	African National Congress
&	and
&Sum	and some
AnE	any
AnE1OutThre?	anyone out there?
AnENews4Me?	have you got any news/information/gossip for me
Anhyd	anhydrous
ANI	automatic number identification
ANLP	Association for Neuro-Linguistic Programming

ANNIE Application of Neutral Networks for Industry in Europe (EU)

Anon anonymous

AnothaDAInParadIs
another day in paradise

Anrk anorak

Ans answer

ANS autonomic nervous system

ANSA Abbey National Staff Association

ANSI American National Standards Institute

ANWB Algemene Nederlandse Wielrijders Bond

ANZAC Australian and New Zealand Army Corps

ANZUS Australia, New Zealand and the United States

AO analogue output; atomic orbital

AO2 as opposed to

AOB any other business

AOBTS all over bar the shouting

AOC age of consent

AOCF Association of Outplacement Consulting Firms

AOCFI Association of Outplacement Consultancy Firms International

AOD areas of doubt

AO/DI always on/Dynamic ISDN

AOL all our love; America Online Inc.; Association for Open Learning

AOLuv all our love

AOM	age of majority
AONB	area of outstanding natural beauty
AOQL	average outgoing quality level
AOR	any old rubbish
AORS	Abnormal Occurrences Reporting System (EU)
AOS	add or subtract
AOTWR	another off-the-wall remark
A/P	accounts payable
APA	American Psychiatric Association
APB	all-points bulletin; Auditing Practices Board
APCC	Association of Professional Computer Consultants
APCUG	Association of PC User Groups
APEX	Advanced Project for European Information Exchange (EU); Association of Professional, Clerical and Computer Staff; Association of Professional, Executive, Clerical and Computer Staff
API	application program interface
APL	Accreditation for Prior Learning
APM	Association of Project Managers
App	apparatus
APPI	advanced peer-to-peer internetworking
Approx	approximate(ly)
Approxn	approximation
APR	annualized percentage rate
APrx	approx (approximately)

APS advanced photo system; Advanced Printing Service (IBM); Association of Productivity Specialists; asynchronous protocol specification

Apt apartment

APt appointment

APT Association of Pensioner Trustees

APW augmented plane wave

Aq aqueous

AQL acceptable quality level

AQMC Association of Quality Management Consultants

AQRP Association of Qualitative Research Practitioners

AR ample room; Arkansas (official postal abbreviation); aspect ratio

A/R accounts receivable

ARA Association of Relocation Agents

ARAM Associate of the Royal Academy of Music

ARCADE Ampere Remote Control Access Data Entry (EU)

ARCHON Architecture for Co-operative Heterogeneous On-Line Systems (EU)

ARCIC Anglican Roman Catholic International Commission

ARD Acquired Rights Directive

ARE acronym-rich environment

ARELS	Association of Recognized English Language Schools
ARET	Association for Rational Emotive Therapists
ARGOSI	Application Related Graphics and OSI Standards Integration (EU)
Arhed	airhead
ARISE	A Reusable Infrastructure for Software Engineering (EU)
ARL	Association of Research Libraries
ARMA	Association of Records Managers and Administrators
ArmCndE	arm candy
ARngmnt	arrangement
Arom	aromatic
ARORL	a representation of real life
ARPANET	Advanced Research Projects Agency Network
ARPS	Agricultural Report Production System (EU)
ARSB	Automated Repair Service Bureau
Artcl	article
ARU	audio response unit
ARU&NP2G	all revved up and no place to go
ARve	arrive
AS	absolutely superb; autonomous system (Internet)
A/S	advanced/supplementary
ASA	Advertising Standards Authority; American Standards Association

ASAHP	as soon as humanly possible
ASAP	as soon as possible; automatic switching and processing
ASBDA	American School Band Directors' Association
ASC	a successful conclusion
ASCII	American Standard Code for Information Interchange
ASCOT	Assessment of Systems and Components for Optical Communications (EU)
ASDB	Asian Development Bank
ASDIC	Admiralty Submarine Detection Investigation Committee
ASEAN	Association of South-East Asian Nations
AsFa	as far
A$H0l	asshole
ASIC	Application Specific Integrated Circuit
A$Kkr	ass kicker
ASL	above sea level; American Sign Language
A/S/L	Age/Sex/Language or Age/Sex/Location
ASLEF	Association Society of Locomotive Engineers and Firemen
ASLIB	Association of Special Libraries and Information Bureaux
A$Lkr	ass licker
ASM	air-to-surface missile
ASmbl	assemble
ASmblPt	assembly point

ASn association
ASO application service object
ASOHD a sense-of-humour deficit
ASOHTP a sense-of-humour transplant
ASP active server pages; Association of Sales Professionals
ASPCA American Society for the Prevention of Cruelty to Animals
ASPIS Application Software Prototype Implementation System (EU)
ASQC American Society for Quality Control
ASSC Association of Search and Selection Consultants
ASSET Automated Support for Software Engineering Technology (EU)
ASSIST Assessment of Information Systems and Technologies in Medicine (EU)
Assoc associate
Assocd associated
Assocg associating
Assocn association
ASSR Autonomous Soviet Socialist Republic
AsSumbdy1nceSEd . . . &IQuot as somebody once said . . . and I quote
ASt assistant
AST Atlantic Standard Time
ASTD American Society of Training and Development

ASTMS	Association of Scientific, Technical and Managerial Staffs (merged with others to form MSF)
ASVAB	American Standard Vocational Aptitude Battery; Armed Services Vocational Aptitude Battery
A$W	asswipe
asym	asymmetric(al)(ly)
AT	any time
at	atomic
@	at
AT11Hr	at the eleventh hour
ATA	achieve that aim
ATA	Aviation Training Association
ATB	Advanced Technology Bomber (stealth bomber); all trunks busy; Agricultural Training Board; all the best
ATBM	Anti-Tactical Ballistic Missile
ATC	average total cost
ATD	actual time of departure
ATDONIt	at the dead of night
ATE	after the event
ATEOEE	at the expense of everything else
ATEOTD	at the end of the day
ATES	Advanced Techniques Integration into Efficient Scientific Software (EU)
ATG	Advanced Technology Group

AthAT   authoritarian attitude

ATHHB   after the horse has bolted

ATIES   Association of Temporary and Interim Executive Services

ATIS   A Tourist Information and Exchange Project (EU)

ATKEM&Ms   at the keyboard eating M&Ms

ATL   Association of Teachers and Lecturers

AtLEstIDntHavAFAcLIkaBmusdHaDck
  at least I don't have face like a bemused haddock

ATLT   all the latest technology

ATM   at the moment

Atm   atmosphere; atmospheric

ATM   automated teller machine (cash point)

ATMDXI   ATM data exchange interface (ATM forum)

ATM-DXI   asynchronous transfer mode-data exchange interface

ATN   any time now

ATOU   always thinking of you

ATR   at the ready

A@TR   always at the ready

ATS   always the same; administrative terminal system; Apple Terminal Services; Auxiliary Territorial Service

AT&T   American Telephone and Telegraph

@T11Hr   at the eleventh hour

ATTAIN	Applicability in Transport and Traffic of Artificial Intelligence (EU)
@TDONIt	at the dead of night
@TEOEE	at the expense of everything else
@TEOTD	at the end of the day
Attn	attention
@TR	at the ready
ATUL	any time you like
ATV	Associated Television
ATWT&BA	all the way there and back again
ATYL	any time you like
AU	audio (as stored computer data); astronomical unit
AUB	American University of Beirut – Beirut, Lebanon
AUBER	Association of University Business and Economic Research
AUDIX	Audio Information Exchange
AUEW	Amalgamated Union of Engineering Workers
AUT	Association of University Teachers
AUT?	are you there?
AUTOPOLIS	Automatic Policing Information System (EU)
Aux	auxiliary
AV	audio/video; audiovisual; authenticity verification; Authorized Version (Bible)
Av	average

AVC additional voluntary contribution (pensions); average variable cost

AVE all valence electron

Ave avenue

Avg average

AVICA Advanced Video Endoscopy Image Communication and Analysis (EU)

AVM Air Vice-Marshal

AVR automatic voice recognition

AVT applied voice technology

AWA as well as

AWACBE as well as can be expected

AWACS Airborne Warning and Control System

AWB Afrikaner Weerstand Beweging (Afrikaans resistance movement in South Africa)

AWHFY? are we having fun yet?

AWOE a wealth of experience

AWOL all walks of life; absent without leave

AWU Australian Workers' Union

AX architecture extended; automatic transmission

AXAF advanced X-ray astrophysics facility (space)

AXBT airborne expendable bathythermograph

AXP advanced architecture processor

AZ Arizona (official postal abbreviation)

B	be
B13	baker's dozen
B24N	bye-bye for now
B2B	back to basics; back-to-back
B2B	business-to-business
B2E	business to employees
B2F	back to front
B2S	born to serve
B4N	bye for now
B5	*Babylon 5*
BA	best available; Bachelor of Arts; Bell Atlantic; business adviser; British Airways; bad apple
BA&F	budget, accounting and finance
BAA	British Airports Authority
BAB	baby
B&B	bed & breakfast
BABA	Blacks Aiding Blacks against AIDS
BABBluii	baby blue eyes
BABDoL	baby doll
BABEL	Broadcasting Across the Barriers of European Languages (EU)
BABIDntCre	baby I don't care
BABItsU	baby, it's you
BABs	babies

BABS Blind Approach Beacon System (aircraft runway)

BABT British Approvals Board for Telecommunications

BABUCnDrIvMyCa baby you can drive my car

BABx2 baby, baby

BAC British Association of Counselling

BAC? by any chance?

BACA business and consumer affairs

BACB British Association of Communicators in Business

BACIE British Association of Commercial and Industrial Education

BACS Bank Automated Clearing System

BACT British Association of Conference Towns

BADAS binary automatic data annotation system

BADC binary asymmetric dependent channel

BAe British Aerospace

BAESC British Association of Executive Search Consultants

BAFO best and final offer

BAFTA British Academy of Film and Television Arts

BAGDA British Advertising Gifts Association

BAGNET Bay Area Gigabit Network

BAHA British Activity Holiday Association

BAIE British Association of Industrial Editors

BAK	back at keyboard; Binary Adaption Kit (Microsoft)
Bak2YaROts	back to your roots
Bal	balance
BAL	basic assembly language; blood alcohol level
BALPA	British Airline Pilots' Association
BALUN	balanced to unbalanced
BAM	Boyan Action Module; Brewster Angle Microscopy
BAMAF	Bellcore AMA Format
BAMBI	ballistic missile boost intercept
BANA	Braille Association of North American
BANANA	Build Absolutely Nothing Anywhere Near Anyone
BANCS	Bell Administrative Network Communications System
BANKPAC	Bankers Political Action Committee
BAOL	British Association for Open Learning
BAOR	British Army of the Rhine
BAP	Biotechnology Action Programme (EU)
BAPC	British Association of Print and Copyshops
BAPT	British Association of Psychological Types
BAR	base address register (computers); British Association of Removers; Browning Automatic Rifle (US Army light machine gun)
BARB	Broadcasters' Audience Research Board
BARCO	Belgian American Radio Corporation

BARD Bodleian Access to Remote Databases (Bodleian Library, Oxford, UK)

BARF Best Available Retrofit Facility

BARS behaviourally anchored rating scale

BARTOC Bus Advanced Real Time Operational Control (EU)

BARTS Bell Atlantic Regional Time-sharing

BASDA Business and Accounting Software Developers Association

BASI British Association of Ski Instructors

BASIC Beginner's All-purpose Symbolic Instruction Code; British American Scientific International Commercial

BASM built-in assembler

BASW British Association of Social Workers

BATB begin at the beginning

BATF Bureau of Alcohol Tobacco and Firearms (USA)

B@TM busy at the moment

BATNEEC best available techniques not entailing excessive costs

BAU business as usual

BAUD a measure of communications capacity, similar to bits per second (from Émile Baudot)

BAWE British Association of Women Entrepreneurs

BB big boy; best of breed; bulletin board

B&B	bed and breakfast
BB4N	bye-bye for now
BBA	balanced budget amendment
BBB	bed, breakfast, bath
BBC	Belfast Boat Club; British Broadcasting Corporation
BBFC	British Board of Film Classification
BBFN	bye-bye for now
BBIAB	be back in a bit
BBL	be back later
BBQ	barbecue
BBRC	Biochemical and Biophysical Research Communications
BBS	be back soon; bulletin board system
B&BS	banks and building societies
BBSD	be back soon, darling
BBSRC	Biotechnology and Biological Sciences Research Council
BBXRT	broad-band X-ray telescope
BC	before Christ
BCAG	Boeing Commercial Airplane Group
BCB	British Consultants' Bureau
BCBC	British Columbia Buildings Corporation
BCC	blind carbon copy; blocked call cleared
BCCI	Bank of Credit and Commerce International
BCD	Bad Conduct Discharge; binary-coded decimal; binary-coded decimal

BCDIC binary-coded decimal interchange code
BCE Bachelor of Civil Engineering; before the Common Era (alternative to bc)
BCECEC British Conference and Exhibition Centres Export Council
BCFG billion cubic feet of gas
BCHES British Columbia Humane Education Society
BCI Battery Council International
BCL batch command language
BCMA British Columbia Medical Association
BC-NET Business Cooperation Network (EU)
BCNU be seeing you
BCOS best chance of success
BCP binary communications protocol
BCPA British Collegiate Parachute Association
BCPL basic combined programming language; basic computer programming language
BCS British Computer Society
BCSC British Columbia Systems Corporation
BCSC British Council of Shopping Centres
BCTV British Columbia TeleVision
BCU big close-up; British Canoe Union
BCWP budgeted cost of work performed
BCWS budgeted cost of work scheduled
BD Bachelor of Divinity; by definition
BD! big deal!

BDA battle damage assessment; bomb damage assessment

BdBy bad boy

BDF binary distribution format; Bitmap Description Format (Adobe)

BDMA British Direct Marketing Association

BDOS basic disk operating system

BDSM bondage and domination, sadomasochism

BDT billing data transmitter; bulk data transfer

BDU battle dress uniform

BE back entrance; below or equal; bill of exchange

B&E breaking and entering

BEAV binary editor and viewer

BEC Bose–Einstein condensation

BECAUSE Benchmark of Concurrent Architectures for their Use in Scientific Engineering

BECTU Broadcasting, Entertainment, Cinematograph and Theatre Union

BEEM ballistic electron emission microscopy

BEF band elimination filter; British Expeditionary Force

BEG big evil grin

BELLCORE Bell Communications Research

BELT bacon, egg, lettuce and tomato sandwich

BEM British Empire Medal

BENELUX Belgium, Netherlands and Luxembourg

BEP	Business Engineering Partnership
BER	basic encoding rules; bit error rate
BERT	bit error rate test/tester
BESA	British Association of Educational Supplies
BEst	beast
BeTaLuvNxtTIm	
	better love next time
BEV	Black English Vernacular
BEZS	bandwidth-efficient zero suppression (telecom)
BF	boyfriend; brought forward
B/F	background/foreground
BFA	British Franchise Association
BFC	bare-faced cheek
.BFC	Briefcase (file name extension) (Microsoft)
BFD	big fucking deal
BFN	bye for now
BFOL	brutal fact(s) of life
BFPO	British Forces Posted Overseas
BFR	biennial flight review
BFrEWivYa<3	be free with your heart
BFT	binary file transfer; bio-feedback training
BFTP	batch FTP
BFTT	battle force tactical training
BG!	big grin!
BGM	background music
BGOd2YaSlf	be good to yourself

BGr bagger
BGT business growth training
BGWM be gentle with me (please)
BH bounty hunter
BHA British Hospitality Association; British Humanist Association;
BHaP be happy
BHD bad hair day
BHF British Heart Foundation
Bhnd behind
bhp brake horsepower
BHQ brigade headquarters
BHRA British Hydromechanics Research Association
BHS British Home Stores
BHSAI British Horse Society Assistant Instructor
BHT butylated hydroxytoluene
BI background information; bibliographic instruction; binary input
Bi bisexual
BIA Bio Industry Association; Bureau of Indian Affairs; Bureau of Indian Affairs (US)
BIAC British Institute of Agricultural Consultants
BIB biggest is best; black is black
BIC best in class
BICBW but I could be wrong
BICMOS bipolar complementary metal oxide semiconductor

BICs	Business and Innovation Centres (EU)
BID	two times a day (medical)
BiDi	bi-directional
BIF	binary information file
BIFM	British Institute of Facilities Management
BIIBA	British Insurance and Investors Brokers' Association
BildrsBm	builders bum
BIMA	British industrial Marketing Association
Bin	been
.BIN	binary (file name extension)
BINAC	binary automatic computer
BINHEX	binary-hexadecimal
BION	believe it or not
BIONICS	biological electronics
BIOS	basic input/output system
BIOTA	Biological Institute of Tropical America
BIOYI/OP	blow it out your I/O port
BIP	books in print
BIS	Bank for International Settlements; best in show; business information system
BISL	Business in Sport and Leisure
BISP	business information system program
BIST	built-in self-test
BISYNC	binary synchronous communications
BIT	binary digit (computer)
BItMe	bite me

BITW	best in the world
BIU	basic income unit
BIX	*Byte* (magazine) Information Exchange
BiZniZ	business
BJC	bubble-jet colour (printer technology)
BK	big kiss
Bk	book
Bkfst	breakfast
Bkgrnd	background
BKOl	be cool
Bksp	backspace
BL	backlit; bill of loading; British Library
BL	belly laughing
BlaBlaBla	blah, blah, blah
BLAISE	British Library Automated Information Service
BLAS	basic linear algebra subroutines
BLIS	Brunel Library and Information Service
BLNDE	blonde
BlOmn	blooming
BlOmnHec!	blooming heck!
BLT	bacon, lettuce and tomato (sandwich); block transfer (instruction)
BMA	British Medical Association
BMBO	bimbo
BMC	British Mountaineering Council
BmClEvj	bum cleavage

BMDO	Ballistic Missile Defense Organization
BMEP	brake mean effective pressure
BMEWS	Ballistic Missile Early Warning System
BMFO	building market-focused organizations
BMI	body-mass index
BMJ	*British Medical Journal*
BMM	borrowed military manpower
BMP	basic mapping support; batch message processing program; benchmark plan
BMR	basal metabolism rate
BMRC	British Medical Research Council
BMSE	Baltic Mercantile and Shipping Exchange, London
BMT	beam management terminal; bone marrow transplant
BMWMOA	BMW Motorcycle Owners of America
BMWRA	BMW Riders Association International
BMX	bicycle motocross
Bn	being
BN	binary number
BN2A	best/better not to ask
BnanaNOs	banana nose
BNFL	British Nuclear Fuels Ltd
BNSC	British National Space Centre
BO	back order; body odour; black out; box office; binary output
BOABB	best of a bad bunch

BOAC British Overseas Airway Corporation (now part of British Airways)

BOAF birds of a feather

BOAGU bend over and grease up (Texan reaction to bad news)

BOb boob

BOB booby; best of breed

BOC Bell Operating Company; British Oxygen Company; but of course

BOD biochemical oxygen demand

BOD biochemical oxygen demand; biological oxygen demand; board of directors

BOE back-of-the-envelope (calculations)

BOF beginning of file

BOF birds of a feather

BOFH bastard operator from hell (may describe your system administrator)

BOGOF buy one, get one free

BOHS British Occupational Hygiene Society

BOIK best of its kind

BoLy Bolly (champagne)

BoLyw0d Bollywood

BOM Basic Online Memory (IBM); beginning of message; Book of Mormon

B0nhed bonehead

BOP balance of payments

BOPD barrels of oil per day

BOPS billion operations per second

Borin boring

BOS Bank of Scotland; basic operating system; behavioural observation scale; British Orthoptic Society

BOSS British Office Stationery Supplies Federation

BOT balance of trade; beginning of table; beginning of tape; robot

BOT build, operate, transfer project (one-off major construction project)

BOTEC back-of-the-envelope calculation

BOV best of variety

Boyf boy friend

BOzBLE booze belly

BP beautiful people; *Blue Peter*

BP blood pressure; British Petroleum; boiling point

bp boiling point

BPA blanket purchase agreement; British Parachute Association; Business Professionals of America

BPD barrels per day

BPFH bastard programmer from hell

BPH benign prostatic hyperplasia

BPI bits per inch; blocks per inch; bytes per inch

BPICS British Production and Inventory Control Society

b.p.m.	beats per minute (music)
BPMA	British Promotional Merchandise Association
BPP	bits per pixel
BPR	business process re-engineering
BProudBLoudBHerd	
	be proud, be loud, be heard
BPS	British Psychological Society
BPU	base production unit
Bq	becquerel
BQ2H	best qualified to help
BQA	British Quality Association
BQF	British Quality Foundation
BRA	baseline risk assessment; Basic Rate Access (ISDN)
BRAIN	Basic Research in Adaptive Intelligence and Neurocomputing (EU)
Brazil	(076) ISO 3-letter country code
BRB	be right back
BRET	best result every time
BRI	basic rate interface (ISDN)
BRI	basic rate interface (ISDN); brain response interface
BRIDGE	Biotechnology Research for Innovation, Development and Growth in Europe (EU)
BRIEF	basic reconfigurable interactive editing facility

BRITE Basic Research in Industrial Technologies for Europe

BRL ballistics research Laboratory

BrLOhEd brillohead

Brn2BMyBAB born to be my baby

BrnBABBrn burn, baby, burn

BrnW/A:-)OnYaFAc
born with a smile on your face

Bros brothers

BRS basic rate service (ISDN)

BRUS boys are us

BS backspace; British Standard; Bachelor of Surgery; building society/ies

B/S balance sheet

BSA Birmingham Small Arms; bovine serum albumin; Boy Scouts of America

BSc Bachelor of Science

Bscn bit scan (computer)

BSDR British Society for Dental Research

BSE bovine spongiform encephalopathy

BSI British Standards Institute

BSOn be soon

BSPP British Society for Plant Pathology

BST bovine somatotrophin (yield booster in dairy cattle)

BST British Summer Time

BSU	Behavioral Science Unit (of the FBI at Quantico); Britannia Staff Union
Bsy	Busy
BSYNC	binary synchronous communications (protocol)
Bt	Baronet
BT	bad timing; Bit Test; British Telecommunications
BT2YaSlf	be true to yourself
BTA	better than average; but then again
BTAICBW	but then again I could be wrong
BTAIM	be that as it may
BTB	by the bye
BTBUCB	be the best you can be
BTC	by the sea
BTDT	been there, done that
BTDTGTTS	been there, done that, got the t-shirt
BTEC	British and Technical Education Council
BTEC	Business and Technology Education Council
BTEX	benzene, toluene, ethylbenzene and xylene
BTF	balance to follow; balance transferred
BTG	British Technology Group
BthD8	birth date
BthD8?	when were you born?
BtmFEdr	bottom feeder
BTP	batch transfer program
BTPON	business telephony on passive optical network

BTR	bit test and reset
BTr1/2	bitter half (husband, wife, partner)
BTS	back to school; base transceiver station; bit test and set; board tracking system
BTSOOM	beats the shit out of me
BTTP	back to the point
BTU	British thermal unit
Btw	between
BTW	by the way
BTX	benzene toluene xylene
BU	base unit; branch unit
bu	bushel
Bu	butyl
BU!	bottoms up!
BUBL	Bulletin Board for Libraries (Janet)
Bu%l	bubble
BUCOP	British Union Catalogue of Periodicals
BUF	British Union of Fascists; buffer
BUFORA	British UFO Research Association
BUKT	but you knew that
BUPA	British United Provident Association
BURA	British Urban Regeneration Association
BURMA	be upstairs ready, my angel
BUS	basic utility system
BuThed	butthead
Butiful	beautiful
BV	book value

BVCA	British Venture Capital Association
BVM	Blessed Virgin Mary (on inscriptions and in epithets)
BVR	beyond visual range
BW	band width; best wishes; black and white; *Business Week*
B&W	black and white
B&W	black and white
BWC	bandwidth compression; Beauty Without Cruelty
Bwd	backward
BWM	block-write mode; broadcast warning message
BW\MIHM	butter wouldn't melt in his/her mouth
BW\MITM	butter wouldn't melt in their mouths
BWTHDID?	but what the heck do I do . . . ?
BWTHDIDN?	but what the heck do I do now . . . ?
BWTHDIK?	but what the heck do I know . . . ?
BWTS	bandwidth test set
BX	big kiss; base exchange
Bx	box
B2X	Binary To Hexadecimal (REXX)
BXA	Bureau of Export Administration
By	busy
BYKT	but you knew that
ByMEtsGrlSOWot?	
	boy meets girl so what?

BYO bring your own
BYOB bring your own beer (or bottle or booze)
BYungBFOlshBHaP
be young be foolish be happy
BZD benzodiazepine

C

c	circa (approximately)
C	see
C	cannot/can't; could not/couldn't
C\\GE	can't get enough
C\\MIT	can't make it tonight
C2D	character to decimal
C4	Channel 4 (television)
C4D	call for discussion
C4M	care for me
C5	Channel 5 (television)
CA	California (official postal abbreviation)
C/A	capital/credit/current account
CA!	chocks away!
CAB	Citizens' Advice Bureau(x)
CABG	coronary artery bypass graft (open-heart surgery)
CABI	Commonwealth Agricultural Bureaux International
CAC	Central Arbitration Committee
CACA	Chartered Association of Certified Accountants
CACD	computer-aided circuit design
CACM	Central American Common Market

CACOHIS Computer Aided Community Oral Health Information System (EU)

CACTI Common Agricultural Customs Transmission of Information (EU)

CAD computer-aided design

CADCAM computer-aided design/computer-aided manufacturing

CADD computer-aided design and drafting

CADDIA Cooperation in Automation of Data and Documentation for Imports/Exports and Agriculture (EU)

CADDIA Cooperation in Automation of Data and Documentation for Imports/Exports and Agriculture (EU)

CAE computer-aided engineering

CAI computer-aided instruction

CAIC computer-assisted indexing and classification

CAIRN Collaborative Advanced Interagency Research Network

cal calorie

CAL computer-aided learning

Calc calculate

Calcd calculated

Calcg calculating

Calcn calculation

CAM computer-aided manufacture

CAMAC Case-Based Hospital Management and Clinical Evaluation in Europe (EU)

CAMAR Competition of Agriculture and Management of Agricultural Resources (EU)

CAMARC Computer-Aided Movement Analysis in a Rehabilitation Context (EU)

CAMCE Computer-Aided Multimedia Courseware Engineering (EU)

cAMP cyclic AMP

CAN Committee of an Advanced Nature (EU)

Cantab Cantabrigian: of Cambridge University

CantWAt2XU can't wait to kiss you

CAP Common Agricultural Policy (EU); computer-aided publishing

CAPD Computing To Assist Persons With Disabilities (Johns Hopkins University)

CAPP computer-aided process planning

CAPS capitals (uppercase letters); cassette programming system

Capt Captain

CAPTIVE Collaborative Authoring Production and Transmission of Interactive Video for Education (EU)

CARICOM Caribbean Community

CARIFTA Caribbean Free Trade Area

CARL Colorado Alliance of Research Libraries (Internet)

CAS	Consultant Accreditation Service
CASE	computer-aided software engineering
CASRO	Council of American Survey Research Organizations
CASS	computer-assisted search service
CASSIOPE	Computer Aided System for Scheduling, Information and Operation of Public Transport in Europe (EU)
CAT	computer-adaptive test; computer-aided testing; computer-aided transcription; computerized axial tomography
CATC!	count all the chads!
CATP	cat among the pigeons
CATS	computer-assisted training system
CATU	Ceramic and Allied Trades Union
CATV	cable televison; community antenna television (original name for cable TV)
CAU	controlled access unit
CB	call back; citizen's band (radio)
CBA	can (or can't) be arsed (interchangeable, but usually in negative); cost–benefit analysis
CBBS	computer bulletin board system
CBC	Canadian Broadcasting Corporation
CBD	cash before delivery
CBE	Commander (of the Order of the) British Empire

CBEMA Computer and Business Equipment Manufacturers' Association

CBI computer-based instruction/instrumentation; Confederation of British Industry

CBIS computer-based information system

CBL computer-based learning

CBMS computer-based mail system

CBOH clean bill of health

CBR case-based reasoning; chemical, biological, radiological warfare; constant bit rate

CBS Columbia Broadcasting System; cost breakdown structure

CBSO City of Birmingham Symphony Orchestra

CBSS Council of the Baltic Sea States

CBT cognitive behavioural therapy; computer-based training

CBX computer-controlled branch exchange; computerized branch exchange

CCC carbon copy; charge card; Competition Commission (formerly Monopolies and Mergers Commission); conference call; copy to; credit card; credit control

CCCP Soyuz Sovietskikh Sotsialisticheskikh Respublik (Union of Soviet Socialist Republics)

CCD charged-coupled device

CCITT	Consultative Committee for International Telephone and Telegraph
CCR	camera cassette recorder
CCTA	Central Computer and Telecommunications Authority
CCTV	closed-circuit television
CCW	counter clockwise
CD	carrier detect; change directory; collision detection; colour display; compact disc
CD	Civil Defence; compact disc; Corps Diplomatique
C&D	collection and delivery
c.d.	current density
C/D	control data
CD-E	compact disc – erasable
CDI	Centre for the Development of Industry (EU)
CDL	computer design language
CDMA	Code Division Multiple Access (a digital wireless access standard)
CD+MIDI	CD-ROM that includes audio and MIDI data
CDOA	Career Development and Outplacement Association
Cdr	Commander
CD-R	compact disc – recordable
CD-ROM	compact-disc read-only memory
CD-RW	compact disc – rewritable
CDT	Central Daylight Saving Time

CDU	Christian Democratic Union
CD-V	compact disc – video
CD-WO	compact disc – write once
CE	Common Era (alternative to ad)
CEDB	Component Event Data Bank (EU)
CEDEFOP	European Centre for the Development of Vocational Training (EU)
CEDR	Centre for Dispute Resolution
CEG	continuous edge graphics
CEI	conducted electromagnetic interference; Council of Engineering Institutions
CELAD	Coordination Group on Drugs (EU)
CEN	European Committee for Standardization (EU)
CENELEC	European Committee for Electrotechnical Standardization (EU)
CENTO	Central Treaty Organization
CEO	chief executive officer
CEP	circular error probability (computer)
CEPA	coupled electron pair approximation
CERACS	Comparative Evaluation of the Different Radiating Cables and Systems Technologies (EU)
CERIF	Common European Research Project Information Format (EU)
CERN	Organization Européene pour la Recherche Nucléaire

Cert certificate

CEST Central Europe Summer Time

CET Central Europe Time; Common External Tariff (EU)

CF cash flow; clever fucker; cost and freight; cystic fibrosis

C&F cost and freight

cf. compare (Latin *confer*)

CFB Canadian forces base

CFC chlorofluorocarbon

CFD call for discussion

CFE College of Further Education

CFI corporate finance issues; cost, freight and insurance

CFM Code Fragment Manager (Macintosh); cubic feet per minute

CFMEU Construction, Forestry, Mining and Energy Union

CFP Common Fisheries Policy (EU); computerized facial recognition

CFR constant failure rate

CFSP Common Foreign and Security Policy (EU)

CG captain general; coastguard; Coldstream Guards; Consul General

cg centigram; centre of gravity

CG control gate

CGA colour graphics adapter

CGE	can't get enough; common graphics environment
CGI	common gateway interface; computer-generated images; computer graphics interface
CGIAR	Consultative Group on International Agricultural Research
CGLI	City and Guilds of London Institute
CGM	Conspicuous Gallantry Medal
cGMP	cyclic GMP
CGS	centimetre-gram-second; Chief of General Staff
CGT	capital gains tax
CGTSTD	can't get the staff these days
CGWS	City and Guild Work Study
CH	clearing house; Companion of Honour
CHA	Corporate Hospitality Association
CHAPS	Clearing House Automated Clearance System
CHAR	character
CHAT	conversational hypertext access technology (Internet)
CHC	cohabiting couple
chem.	chemical(ly), chemistry
CHIC	Community Health Information Classification and Coding (EU)
CHIEF	Customs Handling of Import and Export Freight (EU)

CHIPS	Clearing House Interbank Payments System
.CHK	CHKDSK (file name extension)
CHOHW	come hell or high water
ChPn	chairperson
Chq	cheque
CHRISTINE	Characteristics and Requirements of Information Systems based on Traffic Data in an Integrated Network Environment (EU)
CHTML	compressed HTML
CHUR	see how you are
CHYA!	chill ya!
CI	Channel Islands; configuration interaction
Ci	curie
C&I	cost and insurance
CIA	Central Intelligence Agency
CIArb	Chartered Institute of Arbitrators
CIB	Chartered institute of Bankers
CIBC	Canadian Imperial Bank of Commerce
CIBSE	Chartered Institution of Building Services Engineers
CID	Centre for Information and Documentation (EU); Criminal Investigation Department
CIH	cash in hand
CII	Chartered Insurance Institute
CIIC	see if I care

CIM Chartered Institute of Marketing; common information model; CompuServe Information Manager; computer-integrated manufacturing

CIMA Chartered Institute of Management Accountants

CIO chief information officer; Congress of Industrial Organizations; cut it out

CIOB Chartered Institute of Building

CIP cataloguing in publication

CIPFA Chartered Institute of Public Finance and Accountancy

CIPS Chartered Institute of Purchasing and Supply

CIRC Cross Interleaved Reed-Solomon Code

CIRD Interservice Committee for Research and Development (EU)

CIRIA Construction Industry Research and Information Association

CIS Commonwealth of Independent States; Institute of Chartered Secretaries and Administrators

CISC complex instruction-set computing

CIT Chartered Institute of Transport; computer-integrated telephony

CITB Construction Industry Training Board

CIVR computer and interactive voice response

CIW certified internet webmaster

CIX	Commercial Internet Exchange; Compulink Information Exchange
CKD	completely knocked down
CLAB	crying like a baby
Cld	could
Cld9	cloud 9
CldItBMgic?	could it be magic?
Clevr&GOdLOkin!	clever and good looking!
clin.	clinical(ly)
CLnt	cell-net (phone)
.CLP	clipboard (file name extension) (Windows)
CLR	capital–labour ratio
CLS	clear screen
CLT	clear the decks
CLV	constant linear velocity
cm	centimetre
CM	check mate; Congregation of the Mission
CM?	c'est moi?
CMAR	Control of Misleading Advertisements Regulations (1988)
CMBR	cosmic microwave background radiation
CM-cellulose	carboxymethyl cellulose
.CMD	command (file name extension)
CMF	creative music format
CMIIW	correct me if I'm wrong
CMIP	common management information protocol

CMIS	common management information services/system
CMLB	call me later, baby
CMY	cyan-magenta-yellow (colour model)
CMYK	cyan-magenta-yellow-black (colour model)
Cn	seeing
Cn	cannot/can't
CNAA	Council for National Academic Awards
CNC	computerized numerical control
CND	Campaign for Nuclear Disarmament
CNDA	Community and District Nursing Association
CNDO	complete neglect of differential overlap
CNE	certified netware engineer
CNES	Centre National d'Espace
Cngrtultns	congratulations
CnIFlrtWivU?	can I flirt with you?
CNMB	Central Nuclear Measurements Bureau (EU)
CNS	central nervous system
CNSB	Commissione Nazionale per la Società a la Borse (Italian stock market)
Cnt23	count to three
CntGtEnufOfU	can't get enough of you
CntHlpFLinInLuvWivU	can't help falling in love with you
CntHlpFLnInLuvWivUALOvaAgn	can't help falling in love with you all over again

Co	company
CO	cuddle on; central office; command output; convert out; Colorado (official postal abbreviation); commanding officer
CoA	coenzyme A
COAX	coaxial cable
COB	Commission des Opérations de Bourse (French stock market)
.COB	COBOL source code (file name extension)
COBE	Cosmic Background Explorer (satellite)
COBOL	Common Business Oriented Language
COBRA	Copenhagen, Brussels, Amsterdam (group of artists, founded in 1948 in Paris)
CoC	Chamber of Commerce
CoCom	Coordinating Committee on Multilateral Export Controls
COCOS	Components for Future Computing Systems (EU)
COD	cash (collect in US) on delivery; chemical oxygen demand
CODASYL	Conference on Data System Languages (Group that designed COBOL)
CODE	client-server open development environment; Corporate Outplacement Declaration of Ethics
CODEC	coder/decoder; compression/decompression

CODEST	Committee for the European Development of Science and Technology (EU)
coeff	coefficient
COEM	commercial original equipment manufacturer
CofB	could have ('of') been
COFF	Common Object File Format (Unix)
CoHSE	Confederation of Health Service Employees (merged with others to form Unison)
COI	Central Office of Information
COkBOk	cook book
COl	cool
COL	cost of living
COlB!	Cool Britannia!
COLD	computer output to laser disk
COlTOl	cool tool
Com	commercial(ly)
.COM	command (file name extension); commercial business (domain name) (Internet)
COM1	first serial port (asynchronous port)
COM2	second serial port
COM3	third serial port
COM4	fourth serial port
COMANDOS	Construction and Management of Distributed Office Systems (EU)
COMDEX	Computer Dealers' Exposition
COMECON	Council for Mutual Economic Assistance
COMEDI	Commerce Electronic Data Interchange (EU)

COMET	Cornell Macintosh Terminal Emulator
COMETT	Community Programme for Education and Training in Technology (EU)
COMM	communications
Compd	compound
Compn	composition
COMSAT	Communications Satellite Corporation
CON	console (includes Keyboard and Screen)
ConA	concanavalin A
Conc	concentrate
Concd	concentrated
Concg	concentrating
CONCISE	Concise Networks' Central Information Service for Europe (EU)
Concn	concentration
COND	condition
Cond	conductivity
CONFIG	configuration
Const	constant
Contg	containing
CONTONE	continuous tone
.COOP	cooperatives-business (domain name) (Internet)
COPENUR	The Standing Committee on Uranium Enrichment (EU)
cor	corrected

CORDIS Community Research and Development Information Service (EU)

CORE Congress of Racial Equality

CORECOM ad hoc Advisory Committee on the Reprocessing of Irradiated Nuclear Fuels (EU)

CoREN Corporation for Research and Enterprise Network

COREPER Committee of Permanent Representatives (EU)

COREU European Correspondence, a telex network (EU)

Corrie *Coronation Street*

COS compatible operating system

COSHH Control of Substances Hazardous to Health

COSINE Cooperation for Open Systems Interconnection Networking in Europe (EU)

COSIT Computer Services Industry Training Council

COSMIC Computer Software Management and Information Center (NASA)

COSMOS Cost Management with Metrics of Specification (EU)

COST European Cooperation in the Field of Scientific and Technical Research (EU)

COT cuddle on tight(ly)

COTF concentrate on the future

COTS commercial off-the-shelf (software)

CP	chemically pure; Congregation of the Passion; copy protected
c.p.	candlepower
CPA	coherent potential approximation
CPAG	Child Poverty Action Group
CPI	characters per inch; clock per instruction; Common Programming Interface (IBM); Consumer Price Index
Cpl	Corporal
CPM	control program monitor
CPO	compulsory purchase order
CPR	cardiopulmonary resuscitation
CPS	characters per second; cycles per second; Crown Prosecution Service
cps	cycles per second
CPU	central processing unit
CQSA	Chartered Quantity Surveying Association
CR	credit
CRA	Cranfield Management Association
CRAFT	Cooperative Research Action for Technology (EU)
CRAM	Cyberspatial Reality Advancement Movement
CRC	cyclic redundancy checking
CRD	Collective Redundancies Directive
CRE	Commission for Racial Equality

CREN	Computer Research Education Network; Corporation for Research and Education Networking
CrEp	creep
CrE8YON	create your own newspaper
crit	critical
CRM	customer relationship management
CRO	cathode-ray oscilloscope
CrO12BKInd	cruel to be kind
CROW	Conditions of Roads and Weather (EU)
CRT	cathode-ray tube
CRUD	create, retrieve, update, delete
Crwl	crawl
Cryst	crystalline
Crystd	crystallized
Crystg	crystallizing
Crystn	crystallization
CS	chickenshit
C/S	client/server
CSA	common sense advice; Computer Services Association
CSD	Chartered Society of Designers
CSF	cerebrospinal fluid
CSG	chuckle, snigger, grin
CSIRO	Commonwealth Scientific and Industrial Research Organization
CSL	computer sensitive language

CSLIP	compressed serial line interface protocol (Internet)
CSMTS	Card Setting Machine Tenters' Society
CSNET	Computer Science Network
CSO	Central Statistical Office; colour separation overlay
CSOS	cornerstone of society
CSP	Chartered Society of Physiotherapy
CSSA	Computer Services and Software Association
CS/SS	card service/socket service
CST	Central Standard Time
CSTA	computer-supported telephony applications
CSThnknAU	can't stop thinking about you
CSU	channel service/switching unit
CT	Central Time; Connecticut (official postal abbreviation)
CTC	channel to channel; Children's Tax Credit
CTCP	client-to-client protocol
CTE	cost(ing) the Earth
CTF	City Trainer Forum
CTI	computer-telephony integration; Confederation of Trade and Industry
CTMO	Community Trade Mark Office (EU)
CTRL	control
CTS	clear to send
CTT	capital transfer tax
CTTM	City Code on Takeovers and Mergers

CU see you
CU@TGim see you at the gym
CU2NIt@8YaPlAc?

see you tonight at eight, your place?
CUA see you again/around
CUBE Concertation Unit for Biotechnology in
Europe (EU)
CUC called-up capital
Cud could
CUD? can you dance?
CUI character-oriented user interface; Common
User Interface (IBM)
CUIC see you in court
CUIMD see you in my dreams
CUL see you later
CUL8r see you later
Cum come
Cum2gthaRItNow

come together right now
CUMIT? can you make it tonight?
CUO see you online
CUOnEzESt see you on easy street
CUP Cambridge University Press
.CUR cursor (file name extension)
CURA cover your arse
CUS see you soon
CUSTL8r see you some time later

CUSTS	see you some time soon
CUT	see you there
CUTAH?	can't you take a hint?
CV	curriculum vitae; cultivar
CVGA	colour video graphics array
CVIA	Computer Virus Industry Association
CVO	Commander of the Royal Victorian Order
CW	clockwise
C&W	country and western (music)
CW2CU	can't wait to see you
CW2CUL8R	can't wait to see you later!
CW2HU	can't wait to hold you
CWA	County Women's Association
CWOT	complete waste of time
CWS	Cooperative Wholesale Society
cwt	hundred weight
CWU	Communication Workers' Union
CWUAS	chat with you again soon
CWUL8r	chat with you later
CY	see you
CYA	see you
CYAMIT?	can you make it tonight?
CYD?	can you dance?
CYRS	cover your arse
CYWU	Community and Youth Workers' Union
Cz	czar

D did not/didn't

D do not/don't

D4LA disenhanced four-letter acronym (that is, a TLA/3LA)

D8 date

DA2DA day to day, day-to-day

DAA & QMG Deputy Assistant Adjutant and Quartermaster-General

DAB digital audio broadcasting

DAC digital-to-analogue converter

DACAR Data Acquisition and Communication Techniques and their Assessment for Road Transport (EU)

DAD dispense as directed

DA day; definite article; delayed action; dollar account

D–A digital-to-analogue

DAGMAR defining advertising goals for measured advertising response (marketing model)

DAPS direct-access programming system

DAQMG Deputy Assistant Quartermaster-General

DAr2BDFrnt dare to be different

DAS do a shop

DAT digital audio tape

DATACOM	data communications
Datacom	data communications
Datacor	data correction
Datanet	data network
Datap	data transmission and processing
DAV	digital audio-video
DAVB	digital audio and video broadcasting
DAVIC	Digital Audio-Visual Council
DB	database; data buffer; device bay; dirtbag
dB	decibel(s)
DBA	Design Business Association; doing business as
.dba	date book archive (file name extension)
D\BAF	don't be a fool
DBC	death by chocolate
DBE	Dame Commander (of the Order of the) British Empire
DBIS	Dun & Bradstreet Information Services
DBM	database manager
DBME	database management environment
DBMS	data base management system
DBNO	down but not out
DBS	database server; direct-broadcast satellite; DOS boot record
D\BST	don't be so tight
DBV	digital broadcast video

DC   debit card; Detective Constable; direct current; District of Columbia

DCAM   digital camera; direct chip attach module

DCCI   Dorset Chamber of Commerce and Industry

DCD   data-carrier detect

DCF   discounted cash flow

DCI   Detective Chief Inspector

DCM   Distinguished Conduct Medal; do call me

D\CM   don't call me

DCMAT   do call me any time

DCMG   Dame Commander of (the Order of) St Michael and St George

DCVO   Dame Commander of the Royal Victorian Order

DD   different dimension; Doctor of Divinity; due date

D&D   death and destruction/decay; drunk and disorderly

DD?   what's today's date?

DDB   device dependent bitmap

DDD   decisions, decisions, decisions

DDI   digital data indicator

D\DITP   don't dwell in the past

DDL   data definition language; digital data link

DdntIBloYaMndThsTlm?   didn't I blow your mind this time?

DdntWeGo2DfrtSchls?
didn't we go to different schools?
DDO daily dose/digest of
DDP digital data processor
DDSS different day, same shit
DDT dichlorodiphenyltrichloroethane

DdUHrtYaslfWenUFeLFrmHvn?
did you hurt yourself when you fell from heaven?
DE Delaware (official postal abbreviation)
DofE Department of Energy
DEA Drug Enforcement Administration (US)
DEAE-cellulose diethylaminoethyl cellulose
DEC Digital Equipment Corporation
Decomp decompose
Decompd decomposed
Decompg decomposing
Decompn decomposition
DECT Digital European Cordless Telecommunications (EU)
Defrag defragment
Degrdn degradation
DEK data encryption key
Del delete
DELTA Developing European Learning through Technological Advance (EU)

DEMETER Digital Electronic Mapping of European Territory (EU)

DEp deep

DEP European Depository Library, holdings of EC documents intended more for use by the general public (EU)

DEpr deeper

Deriv derivative

DES Data Encryption Standard

Det determine

Detd determined

Detg determining

Detn determination

DF damage free

DFC Distinguished Flying Cross

DFDR digital flight data recorder

DfEE Department for Education and Employment

DFLA disenhanced four-letter acronym (that is, a TLA/3LA)

DFM Distinguished Flying Medal

Dfnt definite

Dfntly definitely

DG director general

DGAWU don't get all worked up

Dgbrth dogbreath

DGMAAN don't give me an answer now

DGT don't go there

D\GTT2T	don't give them time to think
DGTT2T	don't give them time to think
DH	dickhead
DHE	data-handling equipment
DHTML	dynamic HTML
DI	Detective Inspector; different ideas; district inspector (taxes); do it; dying intestate
D&I	drunk and incapable
DIA	Defense Intelligence Agency (US)
diam	diameter
DIANE	Development of an Automat Integrated System of Neutronography (EU)
DIDAMES	Distributed Industrial Design and Manufacturing of Electronic Subassemblies (EU)
DIDO	data input, data output
DIF	data interchange format
DIKU?	do I know you?
Dil	dilute
Dild	diluted
Dilg	diluting
Diln	dilution
DILY	darling, I love you
DIM	diatomics-in-molecules
DIME	Development of Integrated Monetary Electronics (EU)
DIMPE	Distributed Integrated Multimedia Publishing Environment (EU)

DIMUN	Distributed International Manufacturing (EU)
DIN	data identification number
DINKIES	(people with) dual income, no kids
DIP	Document Image Processing
DipEd	Diploma in Education
Dir	director(y)
DIRAC	Database for Reliability Calculations (EU)
DISA	Data Interchange Standards Association; Direct Inward System Access
DISNET	Domain-Independent Information Services Network (EU)
Dissoc	dissociate
Dissocd	dissociated
Dissocg	dissociating
Dissocn	dissociation
Distd	distilled
Distg	distilling
Distn	distillation
DITYID?	did I tell you I'm distressed?
DiVE	divvy
DIY	do-it-yourself
DJ	disc jockey; desk jockey
DJ2C	don't jump to conclusions
DK	don't know
DKST	don't keep saying that
DL	damage limitation; data link; dead letter/link
dl	decilitre(s)

DL	download (also d/l)
DLD	deadline date
DLG	devilish little grin
DLitt	Doctor of Letters (Latin, *Doctor Litterarum*)
DLL	dynamic link library
DLM!	don't lecture me!
DLS	Data Link Switching (IBM)
DLTBBB	don't let the bed bugs bite
DLTBGUD	don't let the bastards (b'ds) grind you down
DMA	Direct Marketing Association
DMF	dimethylformamide
DMI	desktop management interface; don't mention it
DMP	design-making process
DMs	Doc Martens
DMSO	dimethyl sulphoxide
DMTW	don't mention the war
DMY	day month year
DMZ	demilitarized zone
DNA	deoxyribonucleic acid; development-needs analysis
DNA	do/did not answer
DNase	deoxyribonuclease
DngBt	dingbat
DNIS	dialled number identification service
DNLA	Discovery of Natural Latent Ability
D-Note	500-dollar bill (US)

DNS	domain name server/system
DntArgu	don't argue
DntAsk	don't ask
DntBCrOlWenLuvTrnsBd	
	don't be cruel when love turns bad
DntBSq	don't be square
DntSht	don't shout
DntSwr	don't swear
DntUNoMeFrmSumwer	
	don't you know me from somewhere
do	ditto (the same)
DOA	dead on arrival; drunk on arrival
DOB	date of birth
DOD	date of death/disease
DoH	ditto (the same) here
Doin	doing
DOMIS	Directory of Materials Data Information Services (EU)
DoN	doing
DoNEthngUWan2Do	
	do anything you want to do
DOr	door
DOS	disk operating system
DoUACpt	do you accept?
DoUAgrE?	do you agree?
DoUCmHrOftn?	do you come here often?

DoUEvnNoWotThtMEns?
do you even know what that means?
DoUMndIfIFntsizAbtU?
do you mind if I fantasize about you?
DoUMndIfIStrAtU4Amin?IWan2RmbaYaFAc4MyDrms
do you mind if I stare at you for a minute? I
want to remember your face for my dreams.
DoUWan2SngOrShldISaSry?
do you want to snog or should I apologize?
DoWotUDo2Me do what you do to me
DP data processing
d.p. degree of polymerization
DP! don't panic
DPA Directory Publishers' Association
DPI data-processing installation; dots per inch
DPM data-processing management
d.p.m. disintegrations per minute
DPMA Data Processing Management Association
DPOB date and place of birth
DPP Director of Public Prosecutions
DPP director of public prosecutions
DPS dividends per share
DpStk dipstick
DPU data-processing unit
DQ drama queen
DQMOT don't quote me on this
DR debit; debt recovery; doctor

DR?	Doctor Who
DRA	don't recognize acronym
DRACO	Driver and Accident Coordinated Observer (EU)
DrGnMeDwn	dragging me down
DRIVE	Dedicated Road Infrastructure for Vehicle Safety in Europe (EU)
Drk	dork
DrkbrAN	dorkbrain
Drln	darling
DrmaQEn	drama queen
DrmTDrm	dream the dream
DrOg	droog (sidekick)
DRP	distribution resource planning
DrpM	drop 'em
DrwnInInTCOLuv	
	drowning in the sea of love
DS	deeply suspect; Detective Sergeant
D&S	demand and supply
DSDD	double-sided, double-density (diskette)
DSE	data storage equipment
DSHD	double-sided, high-density (diskette)
DSN	Deep Space Network
DSO	Distinguished Service Order
DSOC	don't stand on ceremony
DSP	digital signal processing
DSQD	double-sided, quad-density (diskette)
DSR	data set ready

DSS	Department of Social Security
DST	daylight saving time; don't say that
DSTM	don't shoot the messenger
DT	daylight time
DTA	daily travel allowance; differential thermal analysis
DTB	data transfer bus
DTD	direct to disk (computer); dated
DTE	data terminal equipment; development, testing and evaluation; diagnostic test equipment
DTI	Department of Trade and Industry
DTL	down the line
DTP	desk-top publishing
DTR	data terminal ready
DTRT	do the right thing
DTS	data-transmission system; don't think so
DTT@H	don't try this at home
DTTBABOWTBW	
	don't throw the baby out with the bath water
DUC?	did you call?
DUCWIC?	do you see what I see?
DUHWIH?	do you hear what I hear?
DUK?	do you know . . . ?
DuL	dull
DUN	Dial-Up Networking (Microsoft)
DUT?	do you think . . . ?

DV	declared value; double vision; digital video
DVAOA	déjà vu all over again (as the Americans say)
DVB	digital video broadcast
DVC	desktop video conferencing; digital video camera
DVD	digital versatile disk
DVD-RAM	digital versatile disc-RAM
DVD-ROM	digital versatile disc-ROM
DVE	digital video effect
DvlInDsGIs	devil in disguise
DVM	digital volt meter
Dvors	divorce
DVR	digital video recorder
.DVR	Device Driver (file name extension)
DW4M	don't wait for me
DWB	???
DWBH!	don't worry, be happy!
DwEb	dweeb
DWI	driving while intoxicated
Dwn	down
DwnTIm	downtime
Dx	Diagnosis
DXF	drawing exchange format
DXM	dextromethorphan
DXT	data extract facility
DYaOH	do your own homework
DZ	drop zone

E

E&E experience and expertise

E2EG ear-to-ear grin

E2TO each to their own

E3LA extended three-letter acronym (that is, an FLA/4LA)

EAC European Accident Code (EU); European Atomic Commission

EACRO European Association of Contract Research Organizations

EAGGF European Agricultural Guidance and Guarantee Fund (EU)

EAK everyone already knows

EAP Employee Assistance Programme

EAPA Employee Assistance Professionals Association

EARA Environmental Auditors Registration Association

EARN European Academic Research Network

EAROM electrically alterable read-only memory

EAS Enterprise Allowance Scheme

EAST European Assistance for Science and Technology (EU)

EAT Employment Appeals Tribunal

EATO South-East Asia Treaty Organization

EAVE European Audiovisual Entrepreneurs (EU)

EBCDIC Extended Binary-Coded Decimal Interchange Code

EBCL European Biological Control Laboratory (of the US Department of Agriculture, French Station)

EBE extraterrestrial biological entity

EBIT European Broadband Intercommunication Trial

eBkn e-banking

eBnk e-bank

eBOk e-book

eBOkn e-booking

eBOOK electronic book

EBRD European Bank for Reconstruction and Development

EBTI European Binding Tariff Information (EU)

EBU European Boxing Union; European Broadcasting Union

EC European Community (now EU)

ECA European Commission on Agriculture

ECB England and Wales Cricket Board; European Chemicals Bureau

ECCE Exchange and Cooperation between Culture and Enterprise (EU)

ECCTIS Education Counselling and Credit Transfer Information Service

ECD enhanced color display; enhanced compact disc

ECDIN Environmental Chemicals Data and Information Network (EU)

ECG echocardiograph; electrocardiogram; electrocardiograph

ECGD Export Credit Guarantee Department

ECHO Electronic Case Handling in Offices; European Commission Host Organization (EU)

ECI Employment Consultants' Institute

EC-IIP European Communities-International Investment Partners (EU)

ECISS European Committee for Iron and Steel Standards (EU)

ÉCLAIR European Collaborative Linkage of Agriculture and Industry through Research (EU)

ECLAS European Commissioners' Library Automated System (EU)

ECMA European Computer Manufacturers Association

eCmmrc e-commerce

ECOFIN Economic and Financial Council of Ministers (EU)

ECOIN European Core Inventory of Chemicals (EU)

ECSC European Coal and Steel Community

ECT	electroconvulsive therapy
ECTG	European Channel Tunnel Group
ECU	European Currency Unit
ED	effective dose
EDC	European Defence Community
EDF	European Development Fund
EDI	electronic data interchange
EDIA	European Data Interchange Association
EDIL	Electronic Document Interchange between Libraries (EU)
EDILIBE	Electronic Data Interchange between Libraries and Booksellers in Europe
EDOS	Enhanced DOS for Windows
EDP	electronic data processing
EDPM	electronic data processing machine
EDRAM	eraseable/extended dynamic random-access memory
EDS	Electronic Data Systems (corporation)
EDT	Eastern Daylight Saving Time
EDTA	ethylenediaminetetraacetic acid
EDX	energy-dispersive X-ray (spectroscopy)
EE	*EastEnders*
EEA	European Economic Area
EEC	European Economic Community (now EU)
EEF	Engineering Employers' Federation
EEG	echoencephalograph; electroencephalogram; electroencephalograph

EEMA	European Electronic Messaging Association
EEO	equal employment opportunity
EEPROM	electrically erasable programmable read-only memory
EEROM	electrically erasable read-only memory
EEST	Eastern Europe Summer Time
EET	Eastern European Time
EETPU	Electrical Electronic, Telecommunication and Plumbing Union
EFA	European Fighter Aircraft
EFC	European Forestry Commission
EFDO	European Film Distribution Office (EU)
EFICS	European Forestry Information and Communication System (EU)
EFIGS	english, french, italian, german, spanish
EFL	English as a foreign language
EFMD	European Federation of Management Development
EFQM	European Federation of Quality Management
EFTA	European Free Trade Association
EG	evil grin
EGA	enhanced graphics adapter
EGM	extraordinary general meeting
Ega2PlES	eager to please
EgrOp	egroup
EgrOps	egroups
EGS	everything goes slowly

EHLASS European Home and Leisure Accident Surveillance System (EU)

EI Exposure Index

EIA Electronic Industries Association

EIB European Investment Bank (Luxembourg, one of the EU institutions)

EIE enough is enough

EIIR Queen Elizabeth II

EIMS European Innovation Monitoring System (EU)

EINE4U enough is never enough for you

EIOL European Infrastructure for Open Learning (EU)

EIS Educational Institute of Scotland; Engineering Integrity Society; Enterprise Investment Scheme

Ejit eejit (idiot)

EK everyone/everybody knows

EL employment law; established links

ELDO European Launcher Development Organization

Elec electric(al)(ly)

ELF Eritrea Liberation Front; executable and linking format; extremely low frequency

ELS entry level system

ELT English Language Training

eLuv e-love

e-Luvn e-loving
EM electronic mail; emphasized; end of medium; expanded memory
eM e-mail
EMA Electronic Mail Association; enterprise management/memory architecture
EMA Engineers' and Managers' Association
EMBL European Molecular Biology Laboratory
EMBO European Molecular Biology Organization
EMF electromotive force
EMFBI excuse me for butting in
EMI electromagnetic interference; every man for 'imself
EMIC Export Market Information Centre
eMMe e-mail me
EMOTICON emotive icon
EMP elecromagnetic pulse (nuclear); electromagnetic pollution;
EMR electromagnetic radiation; enhanced metafile record
EMRS Export Market Research Scheme
EMS eat my shorts; European Monetary System; electromagnetic spectrum; electronic mail system; electronic message service; everything moves slowly
EMU Economic and Monetary Union; electromagnetic unit(s)

EMWAC	European Microsoft Windows NT Academic Centre
EMX	Electronic Mobile Exchange (Motorola)
ENCORE	European Network of Catchments Organized for Research on Eurosystems (EU)
ENO	English National Opera
ENOS	European Network of Ocean Stations (EU)
ENT	ear, nose and throat
Enuf	enough
EO	equal opportunities
EOC	Equal Opportunities Commission
EOD	end of discussion
EOL	end of lecture
EOL	end of line
EOM	end of message
EOSP	employee share-ownership plan
EOT	end of thread (meaning: end of discussion)
EP	European Parliament
EPA	Environmental Protection Agency
EPLD	electrically programmable logic device
EPLOT	Enhanced Performance Lasers for Optical Transmission (EU)
EPNS	electroplated nickel silver
EPOCH	European Programme on Climatology and Natural Hazards (EU)
EPOQUE	European Parliament On-Line Query System

EPOS electronic point of sale; European Open Learning System

EPR electron paramagnetic resonance

EPROM electronically programmable read-only memory

EPS Encapsulated Postscript

=FA equality for all

Equil equilibrium

EQUITY British Actors' Equity Association

Equiv equivalent

ER Edwardus Rex; Elizabetha Regina; emergency room (US hospital casualty department)

ERA Executive Recruitment Association

ERASMUS European Community Action Scheme for the Mobility of University Students (EU)

ERC Employee Relocation Council (US)

ERDF European Regional Development Fund

ERDS European Reliability Data System

ERECO European Economic Research Consortium

ERG Existence, Relatedness and Growth

ERIC Educational Resources Information Center (Internet)

ERM Exchange Rate Mechanism (EU)

ERMA Electronic Recording Method, Accounting (General Electric)

ERMES European Radio Messaging System

ERNIE Electronic Random Number Indicator Equipment

EROM erasable read-only memory

EROS Earth Resources Observation System (US Geological Survey); European River Ocean System

ERP enterprise resource planning

ERR Error

ERW enhanced radiation weapon

ESA Environmentally Sensitive Area; European Space Agency; European System of Integrated Economic Accounts

Esc escape

ESCU European Space Operations Centre

ESF European Social Fund

ESL English as a Second Language

ESO European Southern Observatory

ESOMAR European Society for Opinion and Marketing Research

ESOP employee share-ownership plan

ESOT employee share trust

ESOTW every stage/step of the way

ESP extrasensory perception; especially

ESPI European Software Process Improvement

ESR electron spin resonance

ESSENTIAL European Systems Strategy for the Evolution of New Technology in Advanced Learning

ESSEX Experimental Solid State Exchange
ESSI European Software and Systems Initiative
EST Eastern Standard/Summer Time
Est establish; estimate
ESTA Energy Systems Trade Association
Estbd established
ESTD easier said than done
Estd estimated
ESTEC European Space Research and Technology Centre
Estg estimating
ESTI European Solar Test Installation
Estn estimation
ESTSS European Society for Traumatic Stress Studies
ESU electrostatic unit
eSX e-sex
ET Eastern Time; employment training; extraterrestrial
Et ethyl
ETA estimated time of arrival; Euzkadi Ta Azkatasuna (Basque separatist movement)
et al. and others (Latin, *et alii*)
ETD estimated time of departure
ETDrnk&BMeRE42moroUDIet eat, drink and be merry for tomorrow you diet

ETEE	Educational Technologies for European Enterprises
ETF	enriched text format
ETL	European Test Laboratory
ETLA	extended three-letter acronym (that is, an FLA/4LA)
ETP	Executive Training Programme (EU)
ETSI	European Telecommunications Standards Institute
EtTRch	eat the rich
ETUSGICAL	every time you say goodbye, I cry a little
EtYa<3Out	eat your heart out
EtYaslfHOl	eat yourself whole
EU	European Union
EUCLEX	European Cloud and Radiation Experiment
EUCLIDES	European Standard for Clinical Laboratory Data Exchange between Independent Information systems
EUDAT	European Association of Databases for Education and Training
EUDISED	European Documentation and Information Centre for Education
EULA	end-user licence agreement
EURAM	European Research in Advanced Materials
EURATOM	European Atomic Energy Community
EUREKA	European Research Coordination Agency
EURET	European Research for Transport

EURO-AIM	European Organization for an Audiovisual Independent Market
EUROCARE	European Conservation and Restoration
EUROFAR	European Future Advanced Rotorcraft
EUROFER	European Confederation of Iron and Steel Industries.
EUROFRET	European system for International Road Freight Transport Operation
EUROLOC	Locate in Europe Information Retrieval system
EUROPOL	European Police Office
EUROS	European Register of Ships
EUROTECNET	European Technical Network, projects training and information technology
EUROTOPP	European Transport Planning Process
EUROTRAP	European Transport Planning System
eV	electron volt
EV	ever ready
EVA	Evaluation Process for Road Transport Informatics (EU)
Evap	evaporate
Evapd	evaporated
Evapg	evaporating
Evapn	evaporation
EVCA	European Venture Capital Association
EVGA	extended video graphics array; extended video graphics adapter

EvlWmn	evil woman
EvrEbdEWans2BU	
	everybody wants to be you
EvrEbdEWansU	everybody wants you
EvrEBoDsL@U	everybody's laughing at you
EvrEDAInEvrEWA	
	every day in every way
EvrlstnLuv	everlasting love
EvrRdy	ever ready
EvrE1AK	everyone already knows
EvrE1K	everyone knows
EvrELtleThngUDoIsMgic	
	every little thing you do is magic
EvrEMveUMAkILBWtchnU	
	every move you make I'll be watching you
EvrEN&T	every now and then
EvrEThgWLBALrItInTEnd	
	everything will be all right in the end
EvrEthng	everything
EvrEwhr	everywhere
EWC	European Works Council
EWE	every woman for 'erself
Examd	examined
Examg	examining
EXE2BIN	Program used to convert an (.EXE) file to binary
Exec	executive

EXITE	Energetic X-ray Imaging Telescope Experiment
EXMAN	Experimental Manipulation of Forest Ecosystems (EU)
EXOP	Executive Office of the President (US)
EXOSAT	Exospheric Satellite
Exp.	exponent
EXPO	World Exposition
Expt	experiment
Exptl	experimental(ly)
Ext.	external; extract
Extd	extracted
Extg	extracting
Extn	extraction
EXTREM	Extended Relational Model
EXTRN	External Reference
EXUG	European X User Group
EXVOC	Expert System Contribution to Vocational Training (EU)
EZ	easy
EzELIkSundAAM	
	easy like Sunday morning
EZEPZE	easy peasy

F

F2F face to face

F2K first to know

F2T free to talk (a statement of fact)

F2T? are you free to talk? (a question)

F4A free for all

FA fait accompli; Football Association

FAA Federal Aviation Administration

FAB OK (as in *Thunderbirds*); from all backgrounds

FADN Farm Accounting Data Network (EU)

FAO Food and Agriculture Organization (UN)

FAOR Functional Analysis of Office Requirements (EU)

FAP file access protocol

FAQ frequently asked questions

FAR Fisheries and Aquaculture Research (EU)

FARNET Federation of American Research Networks (Internet)

FAST Forecasting and Assessment in the Field of Science and Technology (EU)

FAT file allocation table

fAv favourite

4n fawn

FAX facsimile

.FAX Fax (file name extension)

FBA Fellow of the British Academy

FBI Federal Bureau of Investigation

FBPS Fellow of the British Psychological Society

FBU Fire Brigades Union

FBW! flash, bang, wallop!

FC football club

F&C fish and chips

FCC Federal Communications Commission

FCCA Fellow of the Chartered Association of Certified Accountants

FCCSET Federal Coordinating Council for Science, Engineering and Technology (US)

FCFS first come, first served

FCOL for crying out loud

FCSI Foodservice Consultants' Society International

FD floppy disk; floppy drive; full duplex

FDA Association of First Division Civil Servants (First Division Association); Food and Drug Administration (US)

FDC floppy disk controller

FDI foreign direct investment

FDISK fixed disk

FDR Franklin Delano Roosevelt (32nd President, USA)

FDROTFL falling down rolling on the floor laughing

FDX	full duplex
FEDC	Federation of Engineering Design Companies Ltd
FedEx	Federal Express
FEEA	Foreign Exchange Equalization Account
FEIP	Front-End for Echographic Image Processing (EU)
FEl	feel
FElFrE FElGOd	feel free, feel good
FElLuvCumnOn	feel love coming on
FElng	feeling
FElTNEdIM	feel the need in me
FEnd	fiend
FEOGA	European Agricultural Guidance and Guarantee Fund
FEP	front-end processor
FEPROM	flash EPROM
fermn	fermentation
FEVAYRS	forever yours
FF	fart-face
ff.	following pages/folios; fortissimo
FFB	fixed-fee basis
FFH	friend from hell
FFS	fast file system
FGS	for goodness'/God's sake
FICCL	frankly, I couldn't care less

FIDI	Federation of International Furniture Removers
FIDIC	International Federation of Consulting Engineers
FIFA	Fédération Internationale de Football Association
FIFO	first in, first out
FIL	first in line
FILO	first in, last out
FIMBRA	Financial Intermediaries', Managers' and Brokers' Regulatory Association
FIORE	Funding and Investment Objectives for Road Transport Informatics in Europe
FIPS	Federal Information Processing Standard
FIS	Fast Information System (EU)
FISH	first in, still here
FITB	fill in the blank
FITB(s)	fill in the blank(s)
FIX	Federal Internet Exchange
FKLW	finders keepers, losers weepers
FL	finishing line; Florida (official postal abbreviation)
FLA	four-letter acronym
FLAIR	Food-Linked Agricultural Industrial Research (EU)
Fld	field

FLEET	Freight and Logistics Efforts for European Traffic
FL&FF	footloose and fancy free
FLIinCulrs	flying colours
FLN	Front de Liberation Nationale
FLOPS	floating-point operations per second
Fl0r	floor
.FLR	folder (file name extension)
FLT	forklift truck
FLW	famous last words
FM	family mediation; Field Marshal; frequency modulation
FMCG	Fast Moving Consumer Goods
FMDIDGAD	frankly, my dear, I don't give a damn
FMN	flavin mononucleotide
FMS	flexible manufacturing system
FMTUEWTK	far more than you ever wanted to know
FNF	file not found
FngusFAC	fungus face
Fntastic!TlbsJstMlt	
	fantastic the pounds just melt
FntsIz	fantasize
FO	Flying Officer; Foreign Office; fuck off
FOAD	fuck off and die (go away, please)
FOAF	friend of a friend
f.o.b.	free on board
FOBL	fell outta bed laughing

FOCUS	Forum of Control Data Users
FOD	fax on demand
FOG	First Osborne Group
FOIP	fax-over-Internet protocol
FOL	fact(s) of life
FOlnYaslf	fooling yourself
FOMCL	falling off my chair laughing
.FON	font; phone; phone directory (all file name extensions)
FOOBL	fell out of bed laughing
FOREST	Forestry Sectoral Research and Technology (EU)
FORTRAN	formula translation
FOTCL	falling off the chair laughing
FOWM	Fibre Optic Well Monitoring System (EU)
FP	fixed price
f.p.	freezing point
FPS	foot-pound-second
FR	family responsibility/ies
FRAeS	Fellow of the Royal Aeronautical Society
FRAG	fragment; fragmentation
FRAM	Fellow of the Royal Academy of Music
FRCS	Fellow of the Royal College of Surgeons
FrEFone	free phone
FRES	Federation of Recruitment and Employment Services
FRGS	Fellow of the Royal Geographical Society

FRIBA Fellow of the Royal Institute of British Architects

FRIDA Framework for Integrated Dynamic Analysis of Travel and Tariffs (EU)

Frm from

FRPI Flux Reversals Per Inch

FRS farce

FRS Fellow of the Royal Society

FrskEVxn frisky vixen

FS full scale

FS2S from strength to strength

FSA Financial Services Authority

FSF Free Software Foundation (Internet)

FSGO floating spherical Gaussian orbital

FSH follicle-stimulating hormone

FSK frequency shift keying

FSP file service protocol

FSW full-scale war

FT flexi time

ft foot

FTA free-trade area

FTASB faster than a speeding bullet

FTB free-trade bloc

FTBOM<3 from the bottom of my heart

FTC Federal Trade Commission

FTF face-to-face

FTGF fight the good fight

FT<30MB	from the heart of my bottom
FTK	first to know
FTL	faster than light
ft-lb	foot-pound
FTNIM	feel the need in me
FTP	file-transfer protocol
FTPD	File Transfer Protocol Daemon
FTT	free to talk (a statement of fact)
FTT?	are you free to talk? (a question)
FTZ	free-trade zone
FUBAR	fucked up beyond all recognition (US military, WWII)
FUD	fear, uncertainty and doubt
FUEO	for your eyes only
FURI	for your information
FUW	Farmers' Union of Wales
Fwd	forward
FWIW	for what it's worth
FX	special effects
FYaA	for your amusement
FYaI	for your information
FYEO	for your eyes only
FYI	for your information
FYIO	for your information only
FZS	Fellow of the Zoological Society

G	grin
G2CU	glad to see you
G2G	got to go
G2GG	got to get going
G2SU	glad to see you
G7	Group of Seven (industrialized countries)
GA	Georgia (official postal abbreviation)
GA	go ahead
GAFIA	get away from it all
GAG	good as gold
gal	gallon
GAL	get a life
GALHA	Gay and Lesbian Humanist Association
GAMES	General Architecture for Medical Expert Systems (EU)
GAorStr8?	gay or straight?
GAR	Grand Army of the Republic
GATT	General Agreement on Tariffs and Trade
GB	gigabyte; Great Britain; God bless!
GBE	Knight/Dame Grand Cross (of the Order of the) British Empire
GBH	grievous bodily harm
GBH&K	great big hug and kisses
GBH&KB	great big hug and kisses back

GBIP	general purpose interface bus
GBLF	Gays, Bisexuals, Lesbians and Friends (US)
gbln	goblin
GBS	Global Broadcast Services
GBU	the good, the bad and the ugly
GC	George Cross
GCB	Knight Grand Cross of the Order of the Bath
GCC	Gulf Cooperation Council
GCHQ	Government Communications Headquarters
GCMG	Knight/Dame Grand Cross of (the Order of) St Michael and St George
GCSE	General Certificate of Secondary Education
GCVO	Knight/Dame Grand Cross of the Royal Victorian Order
GD	gold digger
GD&R	grinning, ducking and running (after a snide remark)
GDB	genome database
GDI	gross domestic income
GDP	gross domestic product
GE	global economy/economics
G8	Group of Eight (G7 extended to include Russia)
GEkStnkBrth	geek stink breath
GEM	graphic environment manager
Gen	General

GENIE	General Electric Network for Information Exchange
GenX	Generation X
GEnysMov	genius move
GEO	geostationary/geosynchronous Earth orbit
GESP	generalized extrasensory perception
GetALIf	get a life
GetDwn2BiZniZ	get down to business
GetYaCotUvePuLd	
	get your coat you've pulled
GeV	billion electron volts
GF	girlfriend
GG	good game
GGFN	gotta go for now
GGG	giggle
GGGG	good game, good game
GGN2DWI	God's got nothing to do with it
GH	growth hormone
GHU	God help us
GHz	gigahertz
GI	good idea
GICSOS	glad I could help
GIF	graphic image format
.GIF	graphics interchange format (file name extension)
GIGO	garbage in, garbage out
GiMETSunShIn	gimme the sunshine

GINTRAP	European Guide to Industrial Trading Regulations and Practice
GIPE	Generation of Interactive Programming Environments (EU)
GIPS	giga instructions per second
GIS	Geographic Information Services
GIU	get it up
GIWIST	gee, I wish I'd said that
GIX	Global Internet Exchange
GL	get lost; graphics language
G/L	general ledger
GLC	gas-liquid chromatography
GLCM	ground-launched cruise missile
GldALOva	glad all over
GLG	goofy little grin
GLIS	Global Land Information System (US Geological Survey)
GLOBE	Global Learning by Observations to Benefit the Environment (Internet)
GLoREDAz	glory days
GM	genetically modified; George Medal
GMAL	give me a list
GMB	General Municipal Boilermakers (union)
GmbH	(German) limited-liability company (*Gesellshaft mit beschränkter Haftung*)
GMC	General Medical Council
GMeYaLuvin	give me your loving

GMeSumLuvin	gimme some lovin'
GMex3	gimme gimme gimme
GML	generalized markup language
GMOs	genetically modified organisms
GMRT	give my respect(s) to
GMT	Greenwich mean time
GMTA	great minds think alike
Gn	grinning
Gna	gonna (going to)
GnaMkeUAnOFaUCn\Rfs	
	gonna make you an offer you can't refuse
GngGngGn!	going, going, gone!
GnIU	getting it up
GNO?	(did you) have a good night out?
GNP	gross national product
GNVQ	General National Vocational Qualification
Go2	go to
Go4It	go for it
GOA	glad all over
GOAwALtleGrl	go away little girl
GOBak2YaPlnt	go back to your planet
GOC	General Officer Commanding
GOd	good
GOdblBadTIms	goodbye bad times
GOdGOdGOd	good, good, good
GOdLuK	good luck

GOdLuvinAEz2Fnd
good loving ain't easy to find
GOdThngGoin good thing going
GOdTImsBeTaTIms
good times better times
GOdVIbs good vibrations
GOGOGOGOGOGOGO
go on, go on, go on, go on, go on, go on, go on
GOL giggling out loud
Gonna going to
GOOML get out of my life
GOPIAInTraFk go play in traffic
GOT gay old time
GotTTim? got the time?
GotYaMojoWrkn
got your mojo working
GOWI get on with it
GOX gaseous oxygen
GoYaOnWA go your own way
GP general practitioner
GPF general protection fault
GPMU Graphical, Paper and Media Union
GPS global positioning satellite/system; global product specification
GPSS General Purpose System Simulator
GPU graphics processing unit
GQ *Gentlemen's Quarterly* magazine

gr	grains; gross
Gr8	great; grate
Gr8B	Great Britain
Gr8r	greater; grater
Gr8rGOd	greater good
Gr8st	greatest
GREEN	General Research in the Environment for Eastern European Nations
GRIP	Greenland Icecore Project (EU)
Grmbo	grimbo
GrOp	group
GrO$	gross
GrOvE	groovy
GrOvEBAB	groovy baby
Grp	group
GrpEs	groupies
Grr	angry
GRUS	girls are us
GrwOldWivMe	grow old with me
GS	good service/sport
GSDB	genome sequence database
GSM	game, set and match
GSM	Global Standard for Mobile Communications (originally 'Groupe Spécial Mobile') – Digital mobile telephony system.
GSOH	good salary, own home; good sense of humour
GSP	Generalized System of Preferences (EU)

GT	group technology; high-performance car (Italian, *gran turismo*)
Gta	gotta (got to)
GtaBASn	gotta be a sin
GTASW	goodbye, that's all she wrote
GTB	go to blazes
GTBOS	glad to be of service
GTBWDU?	go to blazes, why don't you?
GtBZ	get busy
GTCU	glad to see you
GTGFN	got to go for now
GtIt2gtha	get it together
GtItOn	get it on
GtItRIt	get it right
GTMU	good to meet you
GTO	Gaussian-type orbital

GtOnUpGtOnDwn

get on up, get on down

GtOutaMyDrms&In2MyLIf

get out of my dreams and into my life

GTREM	going to read e-mail
GTRM	going to read mail
GTRSM	going to read snail mail
GTT	go to town
GTTW	go to the wall
GtUp	get up
GUE	Group for the European Unitarian Left

GUI	graphic user interface (e.g. Windows)
GULO	General Union of Loom Overlookers
GUROHIO	get your own house in order
GUTS	grand unified theories
GV	global village
GV4M	good value for money
GVT	global virtual time
GW	gross weight
GWTOS	go with the opposite sex
GWTSS	go with the same sex
GYaHOMA	get your hands on/off my assets
GYaMOMT	get your mitts off my tits
GYaOHIO	get your own house in order

H!	help!
H&K	hug and kiss
H&Kxx	hug and kisses
H&O	honestly and objectively
H&S	health and safety
H/W	Hardware
H2A	happy to accommodate
H2GN	have to go now
H8	hate
ha	hectare
HA!	hey!
HABABWan2GtLckE?	
	hey, baby, want to get lucky?
HACOlYOl	have a cool Yule
HAGN	have a good night
HAGOdLOkn	hey good looking
HAGT	have a good time
HAGT?	did you have a good time?
HAK	hugs and kisses
HAKxx	hug and kisses
HAL	heuristically programmed algorithmic (computer) (from 1968 movie *2001: A Space Odyssey*)
HaLeLuja	hallellujah

HAM	hydrogenic atoms in molecules
HAND	have a nice day
HaP	happy
HAP	hazardous air pollutant
HaP<3	happy heart
HaPDAz	happy days
HaPANvrsrE	happy anniversary
HaPBday	happy birthday
HaPHolidAz	happy holidays
HaPXmas	happy Christmas
HaPinS	happiness
HaPNdngGivYaslfAPnch	
	happy endings (give yourself a pinch)
HAQT	he's a cutie
HARD	Hardware Resources for Development (EU)
HavAGOd4eva	have a good forever
HavAGr8DA8	have a great date
HavFnGoMad	have fun go mad
HavITRIt?	have I the right?
HAZ	heat-affected zone
HAZMAT	hazardous materials
Hb	haemoglobin
HBH	hour by hour
Hbk	hardback
HBSA	Harvard Business School Association
HbsAg	hepatitis B virus surface antigen
HBV	hepatitis B virus

HC	health check
HCF	highest common factor
HCGE	he can't get enough
HCIMA	Hotel Catering and Institutional Management Association
hcp	hexagonal close-packed
HCSA	Hospital Consultants' and Specialists' Association
HCT	here comes trouble
Hd	had
HDEpIYaLuv?	how deep is your love?
HDIAU?	how does it affect you?
HDML	handheld device markup language
HDPE	high-density polyethylene
hdr	Header
HDTV	high-definition television
hdw	hardware
HDX	half duplex
HE	high explosive; His or Her Excellency; His Eminence
HedAbuvWata	head above water
HEEB	high-energy electron beams
HEl	heel; he'll
HELIOS	Handicapped People in the European Community Living Independently in an Open Society
HEP	hydroelectric power

HerCumsTSun here comes the sun
HerCumTGOdTIms
here come the good times
HEX hexadecimal
HF high frequency
HFH home from home
HFSP Human Frontier Science Programme (EU)
HGANBuT he's got a nice butt
Hgh high
HghNOn high noon
HGNAbs he's got nice abs
HGV heavy goods vehicle
HH double-hard (pencil lead); happy hour
HHH triple-hard (pencil lead)
HHIS hanging head in shame (not)
HHOJ ha, ha, only joking
HI Hawaii (official postal abbreviation)
HIa&HIa higher and higher
HIB? have I been . . . ?
HIFD high-density floppy disk
HIFllr high flyer
HIH His/Her Imperial Highness
HIHOps high hopes
HIL Human Interface Link (HP)
HIMEM high memory
HIPACS Hospital Picture Archiving and
Communication System (EU)

HIPPI high-performance parallel interface
HIRT hold it right there
HITAOME he is the apple of my eye
HIThr hi/hello, there
HITIms high times
HITULThtILuvU?
   have I told you lately that I love you?
HIV human immunodeficiency virus
HJ hungry Joe
HJAM8 he's just a mate
.HLP Help (file name extension)
HldMeClOs hold me close
HLL high-level language
HLLAPI high-level language application programming interface
HlpMeMAkItThruTNIt
   help me make it through the night
HlpYaSlf help yourself
HLS hook, line and sinker; hue, luminance, saturation (colour model)
HLuvWT have love, will travel
HM His/Her Majesty
HMG His/Her Majesty's Government
HMI His/Her Majesty's Inspectorate
HMM8 he's my mate
HMO Health Maintenance Organization; Hueckel molecular orbital

HMS	His/Her Majesty's Ship/Service
HMSO	His/Her Majesty's Stationery Office
HMTDIH2TU	how many times do I have to tell you
HMTMKM	hold me, thrill me, kiss me
HMTMKMxxx	hold me, thrill me, kiss me lots
HNC	Higher National Certificate
HND	Higher National Diploma
Hndbk	handbook
HndK	hug and kiss
HndKxx	hug and kisses
HOD	hunker on down
HOH	hard of hearing
HOHILuv	head over heels in love
HOl	whole/hole
HOldYaHEdUp	hold your head up
HOLLAND	hope our love lasts and never dies
HoLy	holly
HoLywOd	Hollywood
HOME	Highly Optimized Microscope Environment (EU)
HOMO	highest occupied molecular orbital
HON	hour of need
HOpSt	hope street
HOSCOM	Hospital Comparisons (EU)
Hot4U	hot for you
HotLuv	hot love
HOTT	*Hot Off The Tree* (electronic newsletter)

HotX3	(feeling) hot, hot, hot
HowWasIt4U?	how was it for you?
HOYEW	hanging on your every word
HP	Hewlett-Packard; house party; hire purchase; have plenty
HPC	handheld personal computer
HPCC	high-performance computing and communications
HPDJ	Hewlett-Packard Desk Jet
HPFS	high-performance file system
HPG	Hewlett-Packard Graphics
HPGL	Hewlett-Packard Graphics Language
HPIB	Hewlett-Packard Interface Bus
HPLJ	Hewlett-Packard Laser Jet
HplSlyInLuvWivU	hopelessly in love with you
HPnStnc	happen stance
HPOM	Home Page Objects Model (Microsoft)
HPPA	Hewlett-Packard Precision Architecture
HPSIDOC	HP Sauce is delicious, of course
HPUX	Hewlett Packard Unix
HPyNYr	happy new year
HPyXms	happy Christmas
HR	House of Representatives; human resources
HRD	human resource development
Hrdst	hardest
HRG	high-resolution graphics

HRH His/Her Royal Highness
HrHghnS Her Highness
HRM human resource management
HRMS human resource management system
HrsYaChnc2Gt2NoMe
here's your chance to get to know me
HrTDrMMaGtWckd
hear the drummer, get wicked
HS high speed; high street
HSB hue, saturation, brightness (colour model); high-street bank(s)
HSBC Hong Kong and Shanghai Banking Corporation (the 'Honkers and Shankers')
HSE Health and Safety Executive
HsHghnS His Highness
HSI hue, saturation, intensity
HSIK? how should I know?
HSP highly sensitive person; high-speed printer/processor
HST Hawaiian Standard Time
HSV hue saturation value
HTDS Host Target Development System (EU)
HTEI hope this explains it
HTFP hold the front page
HTH hope this helps; hope to help
HTML hypertext markup language
HTTP hypertext transfer protocol

HTTP-NG   HTTP next generation
HTTPS   hypertext transfer protocol secure
HTTPSR   HTTPServer
HU   Hacker's Utility (a famous hacking utility)
HUFIT   Human Factor Laboratories in Information Technologies (EU)
HUH?   have you heard?
HURO   hold your own
H/V   horizontal/vertical
HVD   high voltage differential
Hvin   having
HvnIsAPlAcRItHerOnErth
   heaven is a place right here on earth
HvnIsInYaHnds   heaven is in your hands
HVP   horizontal & vertical position
HwAbtU&IGtOutOfThseWetClthes?
   how about you and I get out of these wet clothes? (after licking finger and touching yourself and her/him on shoulder)
HwDoULkMeSoFa?
   how do you like me so far?
HWI4U?   how was it for you?
HYaS   have your say
Hz   has; hertz (cycles/sec)
HZ57   Heinz 57
Hznt   hasn't/has not

I&0 in and out

I4t I thought

IA Iowa (official postal abbreviation)

IAATR I'm always at the ready

IAB Internet activities board; Internet architecture board

IABC International Association of Business Communicators

IABS I am being sarcastic

IABTI International Association of Bomb Technicians and Investigators

IAC in any case

IACATer I'm a member of the Centre for Alternative Technology

IACMP International Association of Career Management Professionals

IACPR International Association of Corporate and Professional Resources

IACpt I accept

IACR International Association for Cryptographic Research

IACUC if anyone can, you can

IAD in all day

IADB Inter-American Development Bank

IAE	in any event
IAEA	International Atomic Energy Agency
IAEDB	International Association for the Education of Deafblind (Persons)
IAF	in a flash
IAFAQ	it's a fact
IAgrE	I agree; Institution of Agricultural Engineers
IAILA	I am in love again
IAILuv	I am in love
IAIMing	I am chatting with someone online
IAIMn	I am immediate; instant messaging
IAJOO	it's a jungle out there
IAK	I already know; I am knackered
IAL	internet address list
IALC	International Association of Language Centres
IALUVU	I'll always love you
IAM	in a moment/minute; Institute of Administrative Management
IAMF	it's a minefield
IAMOS	in a manner of speaking
IAMSOProwdOfU	I am so proud of you
IAN	in all night
IANA	Internet Assigned Numbers Authority
IANAL	I an not a lawyer (but . . .)
IANALB	I am not a lawyer but . . .
IANALBIPOOTN	I am not a lawyer but I play one on the Net

IAON	it's all over now
IAP	Internet access provider
IARAW	in a round about way
IAS	in all seriousness; Internet access server
IATA	International Air Transport Association
IATEFL	International Association for Teachers of English as a Foreign Language
IATSITE	it's all the same in the end
IAUP	Internet user account provider
IAW	in all week
IAWk	in all week
IB	instruction buffer
IBA	Independent Broadcasting Authority
IBASS	Intelligent Business Applications Support System (EU)
IBB	Institute for British Business
IBC	Institute of Business Counsellors; Integrated Broadband Communication (EU)
IBD	inflammatory bowel disease
IBElvInMrcls	I believe in miracles
IBElvInMrclsUSxyThng	
	I believe in miracles, you sexy thing
IBetUCntSwmUCldntKEpYaMthSht4LngEnuf	
	I bet you can't swim, you couldn't keep your mouth shut for long enough
IBI	I Believe it
IBJ2T	I'll be just two ticks

IBM I'd buy Macintosh; idiots become managers; incredibly boring manual(s); International Business Machines

IBOMA Inter-Bank Organization and Methods Association

IBR it's been real

IBRD International Bank for Reconstruction and Development (World Bank)

IBRP Institute of Business Process Re-Engineering

IBRU International Boundaries Research Unit

IBS International Business School

IBSA Insurance Benefits Service Association; International Business Student Association

IBTC itty bitty titty committee

IBUD I bet you do!

IC input circuit; integrated circuit; interrupt controller

ICA Institute of Company Accountants

ICAEW Institute of Chartered Accountants in England and Wales

ICAO International Civil Aviation Organization

ICARUS Inter-Urban Control and Roads Utilization Simulation (EU)

ICAS Institute of Chartered Accountants of Scotland

ICAWS I'm chanting as we speak

ICB Internet Citizens' Band

ICBM	intercontinental ballistic missile
ICBO	International Conference of Building Officials
ICBW	I Could Be Wrong
ICC	International Chamber of Commerce
ICC2H	I couldn't care two hoots
ICCC	International Christian Chamber of Commerce
ICCL	I couldn't care less
ICCP	Institute for the Certification of Computing Professionals
ICD	international code designator
ICE	In-Circuit Emulator (Intel); Integrated Computing Environment (Langley Research)
ICE	Institution of Civil Engineers
ICFM	Institution of Charity Fundraising Managers
ICFTU	International Confederation of Free Trade Unions
ICG	Institute of Careers Guidance
ICGE	I can't get enough
IC\GE	I can't get enough
IChemE	Institution of Chemical Engineers
ICI	I'm coming in; Image Component Information; Imperial Chemical Industries
ICL	in Christian love
ICLW\U	I can't live without you
ICLW\YaLuv	I can't live without your love
ICMA	Institute of Cost and Management Accountants

145

IC\MIT	I can't make it tonight
ICnLuvULkeTht	I can love you like that
ICntStndUBAB	I can't stand you baby
ICO	International Committee of the PRCA (Public Relations Consultants' Association)
IConsA	Independent Consultants' Association
ICQ	I seek you (pron. phonetically)
ICR	intelligent character recognition
ICRO	I'm coming right over
ICSA	Institute of Chartered Secretaries and Administrators
ICSH	interstitial cell-stimulating hormone
ICSIC	Integrated Communications System for Intensive Care (EU)
IC**WenUXMe	I see stars when you kiss me
ICTYBIWCYTF	I could tell you but I would claim you talked first; I could tell you but it would cause you to faint
ICTYBTIWHTKY	
	I could tell you but then I would have to kill you
ICU	I'll see you
ICUL8R	I'll see you later
ICUR	I see you are
ICW2CU	I can't wait to see you
ICW2CUL8R	I can't wait to see you later!
ICY	I'll see you

ICYL8R	I'll see you later
ID	Idaho (official postal abbreviation); identifier/identification/identity; inhibitory dose
IDA	Interchange of Data between Administrations (EU); International Development Agency
IDAC	Internet Directory of Advisors and Consultants
IdDW\U	I'd die without you
IdDW\YaLuv	I'd die without your love
IDE	integrated drive electronics
IDEA	international data encryption algorithm
IDES	Interactive Data Entry System (EU)
IDGI	I don't get it
IDiagE	Institution of Diagnostic Engineers
IDK	I don't know
IDKWIG	I don't know where I'm going
IdLOkGOdOnU	I'd look good on you
IDM	it doesn't matter
IDMM	it's driving me mad
IDntACptTht	I don't accept that
IDntAgrEWivTht	
	I don't agree with that
IDntGtIt	I don't get it
IdntI2	I don't intend to
IDNX	Integrated Digital Network Exchange
IDPM	Institute of Data Processing Management
IDRIS	Intelligent Drive for Shop Floor Systems (EU)

IDS Information Dissemination System (EU)
IdSA I'd say
IDTS I don't think so
IE Institute of Export
IE Internet Explorer (Microsoft)
IEA Institute of Economic Affairs
IEC Institute of Employment Consultants; International Electrotechnical Commission
IED Institution of Electrical Designers
IEE Institution of Electrical Engineers
IEEE Institute of Electrical and Electronic Engineers (USA)
IEEIE Institution of Electronics and Electrical Incorporated Engineers
IEHMO iterative extended Hueckel molecular orbital
IEM Institute of Environmental Managers
IEPA independent electron pair approximation
IES Institute for Employment Studies
IES-DC Information Exchange system – Data Collections (EU)
IESG Internet Engineering Steering Group
I/F interface
IFA independent financial adviser; Institute of Financial Accountants
IFAD International Fund for Agricultural Development
IFAL International Foundation for Action Learning

IfAPcturPntsKWrdsThnYCntIPntU?

if a picture paints a thousand words then why can't I paint you?

IFC The internal database of Integrated Information Systems (SII) (EU); International Finance Corporation

IFD image file directory

IFDITD I feel down in the dumps

IFElLIkPGEInTMDle

I feel like piggy in the middle

IfHeDsntShwUpImRtHre

if he doesn't show up I'm right here

IfIamWotRU? if I am, what are you?

IfISdUHdAButifulBdyWldUHldItAgnstMe?

if I said you had a beautiful body would you hold it against me?

IFLD I feel let down

IfPoS if poss (possible)

IFRB International Frequency Registration Board

IFST Institute of Food Science and Technology

IFU I feel you

IfUCntBWivT1ULuvLuvT1URWiv

if you can't be with the one you love, love the one you're with

IfUGtaGoGoNowOrElseUGtaStAALNIt

if you gotta go, go now or else you've gotta stay all night

IfUHdABrAnuUdBDAnjrus
> if you had a brain you would be dangerous

IfUWnt2AMndREdrTherWldBNoChrge
> if you went to a mind reader there would be no charge

IfYaMthWozNEBiGrUWdntHavNEFAcLft2Wsh
> if your mouth was any bigger you wouldn't have any face left to wash

Ig immunoglobulin
IG2TLK it's good to talk
IGA Institute of Group Analysis
IGA integrated graphics array
IGasE Institution of Gas Engineers
IGBP International Geosphere-Biosphere Programme
IGC integrated graphics controller
IGES Initial Graphics Exchange Standard
IGMP Internet Group Multicast Protocol
IGotUBAb I got you babe
Igr8i8 ingratiate
IGWTOS I go with the opposite sex
IGWTSS I go with the same sex
IH in hand
IH2BUWU it had to be you, wonderful you
IH8U I hate you
IHA I hate acronyms
IHE Institute of Health Education
IHEc Institute of Home Economics

IHFU	I have fucked up
IHL	in human love
IHM	I hate mobiles
IHMP	I hate mobile phones
IHospE	Institute of Hospital Engineering
IHSM	Institute of Health Services Management
IHTFP	I have truly found paradise; I hate this fucking place
IHTFU	I have truly fucked up
IHTM	I hate text messages
IHTP	I hate this place
IHTxtMsgs	I hate text messages
IHUHAGN	I hope you have a good night
IHV	independent hardware vendor
II2	I intend to
IIAQ	I'm in a queue
IIARM?	is it a resigning matter?
IIBC	International Institute of Biological Control
IIC	Institutional Investors' Committee
IIM	Institution of Industrial Managers
IIMR	Institute of Industrial Market Research
IIN	it is now
IInfSc	Institute of Information Scientists
IINHINW	if it's not hurting it's not working
IIP	Investors in People
IIRC	if I recall/remember/recollect correctly
IIS	Institute of Information Scientists

IITF	Information Infrastructure Task Force
IITYWYBAD?	if I tell you will you buy a drink?
IJC2SILuvU	I just called to say I love you
IK	I know
IKAROS	Intelligence and Knowledge Aided Recognition of Speech (EU)
IKUHIIU	I knew you had it in you
IKUK	I know you know
IKWYABWAI?	I know what you are but what am I?
IKYABWAI?	I know you are but what am I?
IL	I'll; Ill; Illinois (official postal abbreviation)
ILA	image light amplifier
ILAM	Institute of Leisure and Amenity Management
ILBAT	I'll be able to
ILBCnU	I'll be seeing you
ILBTher4U	I'll be there for you
ILCU	I'll call you
ILDM	Institute of Logistics and Distribution Management
ILKEpYaDrmsAllv	
	I'll keep your dreams alive
ILkeYaCo	I like your company
ILLUIOTS	I'll let you in on the secret
ILLUIOTSIUPN2TNE1E	
	I'll let you in on the secret, if you promise not to tell anyone else
ILO	International Labour Office (UN)

ILOG	Institute of Logistics
ILS	instrument landing system
ILTUWotIWanWotIRLERLEWan	
	I'll tell you what I want, what I really, really want
ILU	I love you
I<3U	I love you
ILUVU	I love you
ILUVUMED	I love you more each day
ILuvUMorThnWrdsCnSA	
	I love you more than words can say
IM	immediate/instant message; Institute of Management
i.m.	intramuscular(ly)
IMA	Institute of Mathematics and its Applications
iMAC	Internet Macintosh (Apple)
IMarE	Institute of Marine Engineers
IMAURO	Integrated Model for the Analysis of Urban Route Optimization (EU)
ImBhndU100%	I'm behind you one hundred per cent
IMBLuv	it must be love
IMBO	in my biased opinion
IMC	Institute of Management Consultants
IMCO	in my considered opinion; Intergovernmental Maritime Consultative Organization
IMDAA	Institute of Management Development Alumni Associates

IMechE	Institution of Mechanical Engineers
IMEMME	Institute of Mining, Electrical and Mining Mechanical Engineers
ImEV	I'm ever ready
ImEvaRdE	I'm ever ready
IMF	International Monetary Fund
IMfgE	Institution of Manufacturing Engineers
ImFrE!	I'm free!
Img	Image
ImGn	I'm grinning
Imgn	imagine
ImGoNaGtUSuka	I'm gonna get you sucker
IMH	in my hand
IMH	Institute of Materials Handling
IMHO	in my humble opinion
IMI	Irish Management Institute
IMi\$MyTDEBerWldUSlEpWivMe?	I miss my teddy bear. Would you sleep with me?
IMi\$nU	I'm missing you
IMi\$U	I miss you
IMi\$U2	I miss you, too
ImINEdOSLuv	I'm in need of some love
IMing	chatting with someone online usually while doing other things such as playing trivia or other interactive game

ImInIt4Luv I'm in it for love

ImLOkn@U&IDntLIkWotIC

I'm looking at you and I don't like what I see

ImLOkn4AFrndDoUWan2BMyFrnd?

I'm looking for a friend. Do you want to be
my friend?

IMLS Institute of Medical Laboratory Sciences

IMn immediate/instant messaging

IMNSCO in my not so considered opinion

IMNSHO in my not so humble opinion

IMO in my opinion

IMOGT in my own good time

IMOT in my own time

IMPACT Information Market Policy Actions;
Implementation Aspects concerning Planning
and Legislation (EU)

ImpoS impossible

IMRA Industrial Marketing Research Association

ImRdE4Luv I'm ready for love

IMRO Investment Management Regulatory
Organization

IMS I must say; Institute of Manpower Studies
IMS Institute of Management Services

Im*vin I'm starving

ImA*vinRtst&IWan2EatU

I'm a starving artist and I want to eat you

ImT14U I'm the one for you

IMTC	International Multimedia Teleconferencing Consortium
IMTV	interactive multimedia television
IMYaDstnE	I am your destiny
in	inch
IN	Indiana (official postal abbreviation)
In2	into/in to
INAOTTFLS	it's not all over till the fat lady sings
INCA	Integrated Network Architecture for Office Communications (EU)
INDO	intermediate neglect of differential overlap
INEdU2NIt	I need you tonight
Info?	give me some information/details
INFORM	Information Management and Decision Support in High Dependency Environments (EU)
INFOSAFE	Information System for Road User Safety and Traffic Performance (EU)
IN\G2SIA	I'm not going to say it again
IN\GUTE	I'm not giving up that easily
INGUTE	I'm not giving up that easily
INI2	I never intended to
init	isn't it
INLA	Irish National Liberation Army
INLPTA	International Neuro-Linguistic Programming Trainers' Association
INMBS	I need my beauty sleep

InMyABCIWldPutU&Itgtha in my alphabet I would put you and I together

IN\N it's not natural

INND Internet News Daemon

INoUR I know you are

INoUR1 I know you are one

INoWenURLIinYaLpsMov I know when you are lying, your lips move

INPO in no particular order

INRI Iesus Nazarenus Rex Iudeorum (Jesus of Nazareth, King of the Jews)

INSEAD European Institute of Business Administration

INSIS Inter-Institutional Integrated Services Information System (EU)

Inslts insults

INT integer; internal; interrupt; international (organization domain name) (Internet)

INTD I'm not that desperate

INTERMAPS Interactive Multimedia Access Publishing Services (EU)

INuUCldDoIt I knew you could do it

INVAID Integration of Computer Vision Techniques for Automatic Incident Detection (EU)

IO information overload

I/O input/output

IOAT	I'm on a train
IOB2T	I'll only be two ticks
IoD	Institute of Directors
IOH4TB	I'm only here for the beer
IOHii4U	I only have eyes for you
IOJ	Institute of Journalists
IOL	information overload
IOM	Isle of Man
IOOH	I'm out of here
IOP	input/output processor
IOSH	Institute of Occupational Safety and Health
IOTT	I'm on the train/tube
IOU	I owe you
IOU1	I owe you one
IOW	in other words
IOW	Isle of Wight
IOWAN2BWU	I only want to be with you
IP	Institute of Petroleum; intellectual property; internet protocol
IPA	Institute of Practitioners in Advertising; International Phonetic Alphabet; Involvement Participation Association
IPC	I'm past caring
IPD	Institute of Personnel and Development
IPhys	Institute of Physics
IPlantE	Institution of Plant Engineers

IPM images per minute; Institute of Personnel Management; Institute of Project Management; interpersonal message

IPMS Institution of Professionals, Managers and Specialists

IPN I'm posting naked

IPng Internet protocol, next generation

IPP internet printing protocol

IPR Institute of Public Relations; intellectual property rights

IProdE Institution of Production Engineers

IPS Institute of Purchasing and Supply

IPSA Industrial Police and Security Association

IPSEC Internet protocol security

IPTC International Press Telecommunications Council

IQ intelligence quotient

IQA Institute of Quality Assurance

IQL interactive query language

IQP2ABOT I'm quite partial to a bit of that

IR Industrial Relations; infrared; Inland Revenue

IRA Irish Republican Army

IRB Irish Republican Brotherhood

IRBM intermediate-range ballistic missile

IRC Internet relay chat

IRC4U I really care for you

IRCA International Register of Certificated Auditors

IRENE Integrated Modelling of Renewable Natural Resources (EU)

IREX International Research and Exchanges Board

IRIS Integrated Road Safety Information and Navigation System (EU)

IRL in real life (when not chatting online)

IRLED infrared light-emitting diode

IRM information resource management; inherent rights mask

IRQ interrupt request

irradn irradiation

IRS Internal Revenue Service (US); Investor Relations Society

IRSYHAFS I remain, sir, your humble and faithful servant

IRTE Institute of Road Transport Engineers

IRTF Internet Research Task Force

IS Industrial Society; information system; interrupt status

ISAALTlPryr4U I say a little prayer for you

ISBA Incorporated Society of British Advertisers

ISBN International Standard Book Number

ISC Imperial Service College; I'm stir crazy; in some cases

ISDN Integrated Services Digital Network

ISdR it's so de rigeur

ISI in some incidences; Iron and Steel Institute

ISM Institute of Supervisory Management

ISMAP	Integrated System for the Management of Agricultural Production (EU)
ISMM	Institute of Sales and Marketing Management
ISnIEr	I'm speaking in Engrish
ISO	in search of; inside-out; International Standardization Organization
ISOTLuv	in search of true love
ISP	internet service provider; Institute of Sales Promotion
ISRO	International Securities Regulatory Organization
ISSN	International Standard Serial Number
IS**WenUXMe	I see stars when you kiss me
IST	I said that; Irish Summer Time
ISTC	Iron and Steel Trades Confederation
IsThtTBstUCanDo?	is that the best you can do?
IStructE	Institution of Structural Engineers
ISUUHAvSchWLPwr	it's so unfair you have such willpower
IT	information technology
IT!	it's torture!
ITA	International Teaching Alphabet
ITAFAQ?	is that a fact?
ItAntOvaTLItsOva	it ain't over 'til it's over

ITB	Industrial Training Board; in the bank; in the beginning
ITCA	Independent Television Contractors Association
ITCLOD	in the cold light of day
ITCOE	in the course of events
ITCZ	intertropical convergence zone
ITD	in the dark
ITE	in the end; information technology equipment
ITEC	Information Technology Centre
ITEOTB	in the eye of the beholder
ITER	International Thermonuclear Experimental Reactor (EU)
ITF	interactive test facility
ITHACA	In-Depth Accident Data Collection and Analysis (EU)
ITHOTM	in the heat of the moment
ITLOD	in the line of duty
ITM	Incentive Travel and Meetings Association
ITMHO2U	I take my hat off to you
ItMstBLuv	it must be love
ITN	Independent Television News
ITNOT	in the nick of time
ITP	in the pink
ITR	in the red; Internet Talk Radio
ITS	in the shade

ItsAMrcl it's a miracle
ItsANuDAItsANuLIf
it's a new day, it's a new life
ITSEC Information Technical Security Evaluation
Criteria (EU)
ItsEvrE14ThmslvsThseDAs
it's everyone for themselves these days
ItsGOd2Txt it's good to text
ItsNowOrNva it's now or never
ItsOnlEAGAmShO
it's only a game show
ItsSoEzE it's so easy
ItsYaDstnE it's your destiny
ItsYaLIf it's your life
ItsYaTIm it's your time
ITT International Telephone and Telegraph
Corporation
ITU International Telecommunication Union
ITUFIR I think you'll find I'm right
ITUM I think you mean
ITV Independent Television
ITVA Independent Television Association
ITX Intermediate Text Block
ITYFIR I think you'll find I'm right
IU international unit
IU2LUVUBIAON I used to love you but it's all over now
IU2U it's up to you

IU4I	I'm up for it
IUA	in your absence
IUCN	International Union for the Conservation of Nature and Natural Resources
IUC\STHTSOOTK	if you can't stand the heat then stay out of the kitchen
IUCWIM	if you see what I mean
IUD	intrauterine device
IUDKIDKWD	if you don't know, I don't know who does
IUDO	I'm under doctor's orders
IUFI	I'm up for it
IUKW2DDI	if you know what to do, do it
IUKWIM	if you know what I mean
IUKWIMAITUD	if you know what I mean, and I think you do
IUR	it's under review
IURA	in your absence
IURG	if you're good
IURH	in your hand
IUSS	if you say so
IUSWIM	if you see what I mean
IUTLUVUBIAON	I used to love you but it's all over now
IV	intravenous(ly)
IvBinWtchnUNotWtchnME	I've been watching you not watching me
IVCA	International Visual Communication Association
IVF	in vitro fertilization

IVR International Vehicle Registration

IvSEnAHeltheaL0kinFAcOnAPIrtFlag

I've seen a healthier looking face on a pirate flag

IvSEnBeTaBoDsInACarBrkrsYrd

I've seen better bodies in a car breakers yard

IvSEnMreHarOnABlyudBL

I've seen more hair on a billiard ball

IvSSILF I've started so I'll finish

IW Internet wars

IW2FUIM I want to feel you inside me

IW2HYaBABs I want to have your babies

IW4gtIt I will forget it

IW\4gtIt I won't forget it

IW\4gtYC I won't forget your kindness

IWADIWAN it wasn't a dream, it was a nightmare

IWan2WAkUpEvrEDAWivU

I want to wake up every day with you

IWANU I want you

IWBAM I won't be a minute

IWBAS I won't be a second

IWBAT I won't be a tick

IWBJ2T I won't be two ticks

IWBNI it would be nice if

IWEM Institution of Water and Environmental Management

IWIK I wish I knew

IWiLSpk2UL8r	I will speak to you later
IWIST	I wish I'd said that
IWITOT	I wish I'd thought of that
IWKUI	I will keep you informed
IWL	I was laughing
IWL&MM8WL	I was laughing and my mate was laughing
IWLAlwysLuvU	I will always love you
IWLD	I was let down
IWldDIHPyIfISawUNkdJst1nc	
	I would die happy if I saw you naked just once
IWLIUWL	I will if you will
IWLMM8WLFF	I was laughing, me mate was laughing. Fucking funny
IWLOL	I was laughing out loud
IWM	Institute of Wastes Management
IWntIUWnt	I won't if you won't
IW\SASo	I wouldn't say so
IWTH	I want to help
IWTHYRBABs	I want to have your babies
IWW	Industrial Workers of the World
IYA	in your absence
IYaF	in your face
IYOGT	in your own good time
IYRA	in your absence
IYROT	in your own time

J	joule
J2LUNILuvU	just to let you know I love you
J2T	just two ticks
JA	joking apart
JAM	just a minute
JANET	Joint Academic Network for Education and Training
JANUS	Joint Academic Network Using Satellite for European Distance Education and Training
JAOTWR	just another off-the-wall remark
JAS	just a second
JAT	just a tick
JBOD	just a bunch of disks (like redundant array of independent disks, etc.)
JCO	just cuddle on
JCOT	just cuddle on tight(ly)
JFF	just for fun
JFK	John Fitzgerald Kennedy (35th President, USA)
JIC	Joint Industrial Council; just in case
JICS	Joint Interpreting and Conference Service (EU)
JIT	just in time
JJ	just joking

JK	just kidding
JKOIT	just keep in on there
JLMA	just leave me alone
JM2p	just my two pennyworth
JOS	jolly old sort
JOULE	Joint Opportunities for Unconventional or Long-Term Energy Supply (EU)
JP	Justice of the Peace
JPEG	Joint Photographic Expert Group
JRC	Joint Research Centre (EU)
JstADrmAwA	just a dream away
JstCLMe	just call me
JstP$nThru	just passing through
JstRmbaThtAnt	just remember that ant
JTJ	just the job
JTLUNoILuvU	just to let you know I love you
JTM	Je t'aime
JTT	just the ticket

K

K thousand; kelvin; knob

K8 Kate

KAIZEN philosophy of constant improvement: KAI (Japanese for 'change'); ZEN (Japanese for 'good'):

KAVAS Knowledge Acquisition Visualization and Assessment Study (EU)

KB kilobyte

KBE Knight Commander (of the Order of the) British Empire

KBPS kilobits per second

KBS knowledge-based system

kb/S kilobits per second

KC King's Counsel

KCB Knight Commander of the Bath

KCMG Knight Commander of (the Order of) St Michael and St George

KCVO Knight Commander of the Royal Victorian Order

Ken trendy plastic-looking boy (e.g Barbie's boyfriend)

KEpOnBlEvn keep on believing

KEpOnBrnin keep on burning

KEpOnPshn keep on pushing

KEpTDrmAllv	keep the dream alive
KFAT	National Union of Knitwear, Footwear and Apparel Trades
kg	kilogram
KG	Knight of the Order of the Garter
KGB	Komitet Gosudarstvennoye Bezhopaznosti (Committee of State Security)
KHz	kilohertz (unit of frequency, 1000 cycles per second)
KISS	keep it simple, stupid; Knowledge-Based Interactive Signal Monitoring System (EU)
KIT	keep in touch
KKK	Ku Klux Klan
KltZ	klutz
KMA$	kiss my ass
KMB	kiss my butt
KMI	keep me informed
KMRS	kiss my arse
KMT	Kuomintang
KndRgds	kind regards
KO	knock-out
KOIT	keep on in there
KOSB	King's Own Scottish Borderers
KOTC	kiss on the cheek
KOTL	kiss on the lips
KP	Knight Bachelor; Knight of the Bath
kpc	kiloparsec

kph	kilometres per hour
KRITIC	Knowledge Representation and Inference Techniques in Industrial Control (EU)
KS	Kansas (official postal abbreviation); kindred spirit
K$nW/Cnfdnc	kissing with confidence
KsRsR	que sera sera
KT	Knight of the Thistle
KUTGW	keep up the good work
KUWTJ	keeping up with the Joneses
kV	kilovolt(s)
kW	kilowatt(s)
kWh	kilowatt hour(s)
KWIM?	know what I mean?
KX	a thousand kisses
KY	Kentucky (official postal abbreviation)
KYaNOOI	keep your nose out of it
Kzn	*kaizen* (continuous improvement)

L	litre
L2BF	learn to be funny
L2K	last to know
L2R	left to right
L8	late
L8NItOpn	late-night opening
L8r	later
L8rD	later, dude
LA	Library Association
LA	Louisiana (official postal abbreviation)
lab	laboratory
LAB	Legal Advisory Boards (EU)
LAB&TUD	life's a bitch and then you die
LAC	Leading Aircraftman; Licentiate of the Apothecaries' Company; London Athletic Club; loud and clear
LACMA	Latin American and Caribbean Movers Association
LAFOOW	like a fish out of water
LAFTA	Latin-American Free Trade Association
LAL	loadsa love
LAmO	lamo
LAN	local area network
LardBckt	lard bucket

LAT	Learning by Advanced Telecommunications (EU)
L@T	look at that
L@TO	late at the office
LAUTRO	Life Assurance and Unit Trust Regulatory Organization
LAVM	leave a voicemail
LAX	Los Angeles International Airport
lb	pound (weight)
LBAC01T	let's be absolutely clear on one thing
LBBB	let bygones be bygones
LBC	legally binding contracts
LBC01T	let's be clear on one thing
LBJ	Lyndon Baines Johnson (37th President, USA)
LBN\L	last but not least
LBNL	last but not least
LBOGE	let's boogie
LBOGEOnDwn	let's boogie on down
LBW	leg before wicket
l.c.	in the passage etc. cited (Latin, *loco citato*); lowercase
LCAC	like chalk and cheese
LCAO	linear combination of atomic orbitals
LCCI	London Chamber of Commerce
LCD	liquid crystal display
LCFC	linear combination of fragment configuration
LCM	lowest common multiple

L/Cpl	Lance-Corporal
LCSP	London and Counties Society for Psychologists
LD	lethal dose
LDC	less developed country
LDCs	Less Developed Countries (EU)
LDR	long-distance relationship
LDRS	life doesn't run smoothly
LDTF	Large Dynamic Test Facility (EU)
LDX	long-distance extender (telephony)
LDYaW	let's discuss your wishes
LEA	local education authority
LEAST	Learning Systems Standardization (EU)
LEC	local enterprise company
LED	light-emitting diode
LEDA	Local Employment Development Action (EU)
LEED	low-energy electron diffraction
LEnOnMe	lean on me
LEO	low Earth orbit
Les	lesbian
LES	Licensing Executives Society
LEvIt	leave it
LEX	lexicon
LF	lady friend
LFA	Less Favoured Area
LGBT	lesbian, gay, bisexual and transgendered
Lge	large

LGS loan guarantee scheme
LGW low-graphics website
LH luteinizing hormone
LHN let's hope not
LHRH Luteinizing-hormone-releasing hormone
LI lending institution(s)
LI2M leave it to me
LIB let it be/begin
LIBK let it be known
LIBOR London Interbank Offered Rate
LIBS let it be said/so
LIDAR Light Detection and Range project (EU)
LIFFE London International Financial Futures Exchange
LIfLuvHaPinS life, love, happiness
LIFO last in, first out
LIfsACnch life's a cinch
LIk like
LIL last in line; let it last
LINAC Linear Accelerator, part of the Joint Research Centre (JRC). (EU)
liq liquid
LISP list processing
listserv electronic mailing list used by discussion groups on the Internet
LItsOnDorOpnNo1In
lights on, door open, no one in

LItUpYaWrld	light up your world
LivItUp	live it up
LJ	Lord Justice
LJBF	let's just be friends
LkEU	lucky you
LKIT	like it
LL B	Bachelor of Laws (Latin, *Legum Baccalaureus*)
LL D	Doctor of Laws (Latin, *Legum Doctor*)
LLL	lay, lady, lay; low-level language
LL M	Master of Laws (Latin, *Legum Magister*)
LLOD	last line of defence
LLOX	lunar liquid oxygen (space)
LLTA	lots and lots of thunderous applause
lm	lumen
LMA	leave me alone
LMAO	laughing/laugh my arse/ass off
LMB	leave me be
LMC	lost my connection
LMD	last man down; last-minute decision
LMI	let me in
LMIOTS	let me in on the secret
LMK	let me know
LMKITM	let me know in the morning
LMMMC	let me make myself clear
LMMMU	let me make myself understood
Lmp	lump
LMS	let me speak; London Missionary Society

LNA	let's not argue
LNB	let's not bicker/bitch
LNGCA	let's not get carried away
LN\J2C	let's not jump to conclusions
L&NL	local and national level
LO	hello
LO!	look out!
LOALP	leaning on a lamppost
LOB	line-of-balance (chart)
LOBL	lots of belly laughing
Loco	locomotive; train

LoILuvUWntUTLMeYaNme?

hello, I love you. Won't you tell me your name?

LOk	look
LOkWhsCmn	look who's coming
LOL	lots of luck; lots of laughs; laughing out loud
LOMBARD	loads of money but a right dickhead
LOnETUn	looneytune
L@@K	look
LOP	last orders, please
LOTJ	law of the jungle
LOTL	lie of the land
LOTP	leader of the pack
LOX	liquid oxygen
LP	long-playing record
LPG	liquefied petroleum gas

LPO	London Philharmonic Orchestra
LPR	let's phone-race
LRAM	Licentiate of the Royal Academy of Music
LRB	liquid rocket booster (space)
LRBM	long-range ballistic missile
LRF	little rubber feet (the little pads on the bottom of displays and other equipment)
LS	large scale
L&S	large and small
LS!	life sucks!
LSB	lock, stock and barrel
LSC	Legal Services Commission
LSD	lysergic acid diethylamide
LSE	London School of Economics; London School of Economics
LSHNPN	laughed so hard new pants needed
LSI	large-scale integration
LSO	London Symphony Orchestra
LSR	least significant bit
LST	let's save time
LstInU	lost in you
Lt	Lieutenant
Lt Col	Lieutenant Colonel
Lt Gen	Lieutenant General
LTA	Lawn Tennis Association; lots of thunderous applause
LTC	long time coming

LTEB	let the entertainment begin
LTIC	long time in coming
LtItB	let it be
LTK	last to know
LtLBtOfHvn	little bit of heaven
Ltle	little
LtLuvRul	let love rule
LtLuvShIn	let love shine
LTM	laugh to myself
LtMeDrwUAPctur	
	let me draw you a picture
LTNC	long time no see
LTOM	London Traded Option Market
LTR	long-term relationship
LTSB	Lloyds TSB
LtsB2gtha	let's be together
LtsCoOp	let's co-operate
LtsGet2gtha	let's get together
LtsGtHaPE	let's get happy
LtsHavABaL	let's have a ball
LTSI	let that sink in
LtsMkThsANIt2Rmba	
	let's make this a night to remember
LtTFlAmBrnBrIta	
	let the flame burn brighter
LtTGOdTImsRoL	
	let the good times roll

LtYa<3Dns	let your heart dance
LtYaLuvFlO	let your love flow
LtYaslfGO	let yourself go
LU	London Underground
LUHN	let us hope not
LUL	love you lots
LULAB	love you like a brother
LULAS	love you like a sister
LUMO	lowest unoccupied molecular orbital
LUNA	let us not argue
LUNB	let us not bicker/bitch
LUNJ2C	let us not jump to conclusions
Luv	love
LUV2TLK	love to talk
LuvIsEvrEThng	love is everything
LuvIsTDrug	love is the drug
LuvMeLuvMyDog	
	love me, love my dog
LuvMeWrm&Tndr	
	love me warm and tender
LuvMnsNvaHvin2SAURSrE	
	love means never having to say you're sorry
LuvOrO	love or nothing
LuvPEs&HrmnE	love peace and harmony
LuvsCum@U	love's coming at you
LUVTLK	love talk
LuvWLCnkrAL	love will conquer all

LuvWLFndAWA	love will find a way
LuvYa	love you
LUWAM<3	love you with all my heart
LV	luncheon voucher
LVO	Lieutenant of the Royal Victorian Order
Lw	low
LW4gt	lest we forget
LwDwn	low down
LWH	long way home
LWI	loitering with intent
Lx	love with a kiss
Lxx	love and kisses
LZ	landing zone

M

m	metre
M3Z	mobile-phone-free zone
M4I	mad for it
M8	mate
MA	Massachusetts (official postal abbreviation); Master of Arts
MAC	multiplexed analogue component
MACS	Maintenance Assistance Capability Software (EU)
MAFF	Ministry of Agriculture, Fisheries and Food
MAIEndThsSntncWivAPropstn?	may I end this sentence with a proposition?
Maj	Major
MAkItEzEOnYaslf	make it easy on yourself
MAkItHPn	make it happen
MAkItREl	make it real
MAkItSOn	make it soon
MAkMe!	make me!
MAkMyDASA+!	make my day, say yes
MAkTWrldGoRnd	make the world go round
manuf	manufacture

manufd	manufactured
manufg	manufacturing
MAO	monoamine oxidase
MAP	making a pass
MAPGGB	mine's a Pan-Galactic Gargle Blaster
MAROPT	Marine Optical Recording System (EU)
MARSIS	Marine Remote Sensing Information System for Regional European Seas
MASQUES	Medical Application Software Quality Enhancement by Standards (EU)
MAST	Marine Science and Technology (EU)
math	mathematical(ly)
MATIC	Multi-Strategy Authoring Toolkit for Intelligent Courseware (EU)
MATV	Master Antenna Television
MATZ	military air traffic zone
MAU	mad about you
Max	maximum
MAX	Metropolitan Area Communication System (EU)
MB	Bachelor of Medicine (Latin, *Medicinae Baccalaureus*); megabyte
MBA	Master in Business Administration
MBASIC	Microsoft BASIC
MBCS	Managed Business Consultancy Service (Chartered Institute of Marketing)
MBD	man bites dog

MBE	Member (of the Order of the) British Empire
MBO	management by objectives
MBR	master boot record
MBSA	Manual Business Systems Association
MBTI	Myers Briggs Type Indicator
MBURBMJ	My, but you're beautiful, Miss Jones
MBWA	management by walking around
MBX	mailbox
MC	Master of Ceremonies; Military Cross
M&C	mediation and conciliation
MCA	Management Consultancies Association; Monetary Compensation Amount
MCACE	Measurement Characterization and Control of Ambulatory Care in Europe
MCAs	Monetary Compensation Amounts (EU)
MCC	Marylebone Cricket Club
MCI	Management Charter Initiative
MCIS	Management Consultancy Information Service
MCP	male chauvinist pig
MC-SCF	multiconfigurational self-consistent field
MD	Doctor of Medicine (Latin, *Medicinae Doctor*); managing director; Maryland (official postal abbreviation); most definitely
MDAL	mutton dressed as lamb
MDMA	methylene dioxymethamphetamine (ecstasy)
MDT	Mountain Daylight Saving Time

MDX	modular digital exchange
ME	Maine (official postal abbreviation); myalgic encephalomyelitis
Me	methyl
Me&U	me and you
Me4U	me for you
MEB	memory expansion board
mech	mechanical(ly) (not mechanism)
Med	immediately
MEDALUS	Mediterranean Desertification and Land Use Impacts (EU)
MEDIA	Measures for Encouraging the Development of the Audiovisual Production Industry (EU)
MEDICA	Multimedial Medical Diagnostic Assistant (EU)
MEDSPA	Mediterranean Special Programme of Action (EU)
MEP	Member of the European Parliament
MERCHANT	Methods in Electronic Retail Cash Handling (EU)
MERMAID	Metrication and Resource Modelling Aid; Marine Environment Remote-Controlled Measuring and Integrated Detection (EU)
MERMAIDS	Mediterranean Eddy Resolving Modelling and Interdisc Studies (EU)
MES	makes excellent sense
metab	metabolism

METKIT	Metrics Education Toolkit project (EU)
mf	*mezzo forte* ('fairly loud')
MFA	Multi-Fibre Agreement
MFH	Master of Foxhounds
MFI!	mad for it!
mfr	manufacturer; manufacture
mg	milligram(s)
MGB	may God bless
MGQ	Maximum Guarantee Quality (tobacco-production statistic) (EU)
Mgr	manager; Monsignor; Monseigneur
MGt	maggot
MH	Medal of Honor (US)
M<3BlEds4U	my heart bleeds for you
MHD	magnetohydrodynamics
M<3GO2U	my heart goes out to you
MHOTY	my hat's off to you
MHz	megahertz
MI	maximizing investment; Michigan (official postal abbreviation); mistaken identity
mi	mile
MI5	Security Service
MI6	Secret Intelligence Service
MIA	Meetings Industry Association
MIBN	Microsoft International Business Network
MICR	magnetic ink character recognition

MIDAS Management Information Dissemination Administrative System (EU)

MIDI musical instrument digital interface

MIM molecules-in-molecules

MIMI Medical Workstations for Intelligent Interactive Acquisition and Analysis of Digital Medical Images (EU)

min minimum; minute

MINE Microbial Information Network Europe

MINT Managing the Integration of New Technology (EU)

MINX multimedia information network exchange

MIOCA Monolithic Integrated Optics for Customer Access Applications (EU)

MIPS million instructions per second

MIRAGE Migration of Radioisotopes in the Geosphere (EU)

MIRAS Mortgage Interest Relief at Source

MIRIAM Model Scheme for Information on Rural Development Initiatives and Agree Markets (EU)

MIRV multiple independently targeted re-entry vehicle

MIS make it so; maybe so; make it stop; IS Management Information Systems

Mi$ miss

Misc miscellaneous

MISEP	Mutual Information System on Employment Policies (EU)
Mi$n	missing
Mi$nU	missing you
MIT	Massachusetts Institute of Technology
MITI	Multilingual Intelligence Interface (EU)
MIX	member information exchange
mixt	mixture
ml	millilitre(s); mile(s)
ML8r	more later; much later
MLB	Major League Baseball
MLLthed	mullethead
MLM	multilevel marketing
MlR	minimum lending rate
MLR	minimum lending rate
mm	millimetre(s)
MM8	my mate
MMC	Monopolies and Mergers Commission (now Competition Commission)
MMD	make my day
MMDP	make my day, punk
mmf	magnetomotive force
MMI	man–machine interaction
MML8r	much more later; much, much later
MMOB	minding my own business
MMOS	Multi-Modal Organ Modelling System (EU)
MMU	memory management unit

MMX	mastergroup multiplex; multimedia extensions
MN	Minnesota (official postal abbreviation)
MNchkn	munchkin (short)
MndBdESol	mind, body, soul
MndNmn	mind-numbing
MNDO	modified neglect of diatomic overlap
MNE	multinational enterprise
MnE	money
MnEMAksTWrldGoARound	
	'Money makes the world go around'
MngBg	minge-bag (miser)
MNM	make no mistake
MNP	Microcom Network Protocol
Mnsta	monster
Mnth	month
Mnthly	monthly
Mnths	months
MO	Medical Officer; Missouri (official postal abbreviation); money order; molecular orbital
mo	month
MOB	man overboard
Mob	mobile; mobile phone
MOB	mother of blonde
MoBDik	Moby Dick
MOBIDICK	Multivariable On-Line Bilingual Dictionary Kit (EU)

MoD	Ministry of Defence
MODEM	modulator/demodulator
MOF	matter of fact
MOH	Medal of Honor (US)
MOI	misuse of information
mol	molecule, molecular
MOM	major or minor
MOMIMTS	Military and Orchestral Musical Instrument Makers Trade Society
Mong	mongrel
MorF?	male or female?
MOSS	member of the same sex
MOTD	message of the day
MOTN	middle of the night; more often than not
MOTOS	member of the opposite sex
MOvnUpMOvnOn	moving up, moving on
MOvOUp	moving on up
MOvYaBdE	move your body
MowsbrAn	mousebrain
MP	Member of Parliament
mp	*mezzo piano* (fairly soft)
m.p.	melting point
mpc	megaparsec
MPDR	many people don't realize
MPEG	Motion Picture Expert Group
mpg	miles per gallon

m.p.h.	miles per hour
MPO	Managerial and Professional Officers
MPTP	methylphenyltetrahydropyridine
MPX	multiplexer; multiplex
MRA	Moral Rearmament
MRINA	Member of the Royal Institution of Naval Architects
mRNA	messenger RNA
MRP	manufacturing resource planning; materials requirement planning
MRS	Market Research Society
MREMe	marry me
MREXms	merry Christmas
MS	manuscript; Marketing Society; Mississippi (official postal abbreviation); multiple sclerosis
MS	manuscript; multiple sclerosis
MSB	most significant bit
MSBF	mean swaps before failure
MSc	Master of Science
MSD	Moscow Summer Time
MSDOS	Microsoft Disk Operating System
MSF	Manufacturing Science Finance (union)
Msg	message
MSG	monosodium glutamate
Msgs	messages
MSH	melanocyte-stimulating hormone

MSK	Moscow Time
MSM	Meritorious Service Medal
MSP	Member of the Scottish Parliament
MSS	manuscripts
MST	Mountain Standard Time
Mstrb8	masturbate
MT	Montana (official postal abbreviation)
Mt	Mount
MT	Mountain Time
MTB	motor torpedo boat
MTBA	methyl tertiary butyl alcohol
MTBCF	mean time between critical failures
MTBE	methyl tertiary butyl ethylene
MTBF	mean time before failure/between failures
MTE	my thoughts exactly
MTFBWU	may the Force be with you (sci-fi)
MTRM	make the right move
MTX	mobile telephone exchange
MU	Musicians' Union
MU?	must you . . . ?
MUD	multi-user dimension
MUMBLE	multiple user multicast basic language exchange
MunE$$$£££MunE	money, money, money
MURIM	Multi-Dimensional Reconstruction and Imaging in Medicine (EU)

MUSIP	Multisensor Image Processor (EU)
MUSM	miss you so much
MUTEX	mutual exclusion; mutually exclusive
M&V	many and varied
MVO	Member of the Royal Victorian Order
MW	megawatt(s)
MWOSTU	my way of saying thank you
MX	mail exchanger (Internet)
Mx	maxwell unit
MXU	multiplexer unit
MYaOB	mind your own business
MYaWK	make your wishes known
MYOB	mind your own business
MYROB	mind your own business
My2¢	my two cents (my opinion)

N

N	not
N1!	nice one!
N2CU2CUN	nice to see you, to see you, nice
N2DBWU	nice to do business with you
N2DWM	nothing to do with me
N2G	not too good
N2H	nowhere to hide
N2K	need to know (basis)
N2MU	nice to meet you
N2N	next to nothing
N2NiteJo	not tonight, Josephine
N2R	nowhere to run
N2T	nowhere to turn
N2U	next to you
n/a	no account (banking); not applicable; not available
NAACP	National Association for the Advancement of Colored People (US)
NAAFI	Navy, Army and Air Force Institutes (servicemen's canteen)
NABIT	not a bad idea that
NACAB	National Association of Citizens' Advice Bureaux

NACGT National Association of Careers and Guidance Teachers

NACODS National Association of Colliery Overmen, Deputies and Shotfirers

NAD nicotinamide adenine dinucleotide

NADP nicotinamide adenine dinucleotide phosphate

NAGI not a good idea

Nak not acknowledged (data transfer)

NALGO National and Local Government Officers' Association (merged with others to form Unison)

NAMAS National Measurement and Accreditation Service

NAMC Northern Association of Management Consultants

NANT not a nice thought

NAOE National Association for Outdoor Education

NAPF National Association of Pension Funds

NAPO National Association of Probation Officers

NASA National Aeronautics and Space Administration

NASDA National Space Development Agency

NASUWT National Association of Schoolmasters/Union of Woman Teachers

NATFHE National Association of Teachers in Further and Higher Education

NATO North Atlantic Treaty Organization

NB	note well (Latin, *nota bene*)
NB2D	nothing better to do
NBC	National Broadcasting Company (US)
NBD	no big deal
NBD	no big deal; night becomes day
NBM	nil by mouth
NBN	naughty but nice
NBPMC	Executive Advisory Board of National Bureau of Professional Management Consultants
NBSP	nonbreaking space (word processing)
NBTCBW	nothing's bad that can't be worse
NBV	net book value
NBVM	narrow-band voice modulation
NC	North Carolina (official postal abbreviation)
NCA	Northern Consultancy Association
NCC	National Computing Centre
NCIS	National Criminal Investigation Service
NCMA	National Childminding Association
NCO	noncommissoned officer
NCVQ	National Council for Vocational Qualification
nd	and
ND	New Deal
ND	North Dakota (official postal abbreviation)
N&D	night and day
NDD	next door down
NDDO	neglect of diatomic differential overlap
NDE	near-death experience

Ndl\$Luv endless love

Ndl\$ endless

NDN next door neighbour

NDoin not doing

NE any

NE Nebraska (official postal abbreviation);
northeastern

NE1 anyone

NE1WHdA<3WldNoThtILuvU

anyone who had a heart . . . would know
that I love you

NEBOSH National Examining Board in Occupational
Safety and Health

NEBSM National Examining Board in Supervisory
Management

NEd need

NEDC National Economic Development Office

NEDO National Economic Development Office

neg negative(ly)

NEH any how

NEM any more

NEPlAc any place

NET any time; not enough time

Net Internet

Nethng anything

NEthngIsPSble anything is possible

NEthngUWan anything you want

NETIm	anytime
NETT	National Education and Training Target; Network for Environmental Technology Transfer (EU)
NEVIS	Neural Vehicle Information System (EU)
NEW	any where
NEwer	any where
NEWn	any when
NEWS	north, east, west, south
NEXAFS	near-edge X-ray absorption fine structure (physics)
NF	National Front
N\F2T	not free to talk
NFC	National Football Conference
NFD	next floor down
NFG	no fucking good
NFM	never works for me
NFU	National Farmers' Union; next floor up
NFW	no feasible/fucking way
NGA	no-go area
NGF	nerve growth factor
NGNJ	no gunk, no junk
N\gonna	not going
NGSU	Nationwide Group Staff Union
NGTCBB	nothing's good that can't be better
NGV4M	not good value for money
NH	New Hampshire (official postal abbreviation)

NH	nice hand
NHL	National Hockey League
NHOH	never heard of him/her
NHS	National Health Service
NI	National Insurance; new identity; *New Internationalist*; Northern Ireland
NI@A	no idea at all
NIC	newly industrializing country
NICCI	Northern Ireland Chamber of Commerce and Industry
NIcDr$CnITlkUOutOfIt?	nice dress, can I talk you out of it?
NICE	National Institute for Clinical Excellence
NIDW2C	no, I don't want to chat
NIFOC	naked in front of computer
NIFOCEM&Ms	naked in front of computer eating M&Ms
NIH	National Institutes of Health
NIJB	*Northern Ireland Judgements Bulletin*
NIMBY	(someone who says) not in my back yard
NIMCO	not in my considered opinion
NIMHO	not in my humble opinion
NIMNSCO	not in my not so considered opinion
NIMNSHO	not in my not so humble opinion
NIMO	not in my opinion
NiMWad	nimwad
NIST	National Institute of Standards and Technology (USA)

NITREX	Nitrogen Saturation Experiments (EU)
NJ	New Jersey (official postal abbreviation)
NL	New Labour; not likely
NLB	New Labour bollocks; never look back
NLBD	National League of the Blind and Disabled
NLI	not logged in
NLP	neurolinguistic programming
NLPAD	Natural Language Processing of Patient Discharge (EU)
NLRB	National Labor Relations Board (US)
NM	never mind; New Mexico (official postal abbreviation)
NMD	National Missile Defense ('Son of Star Wars')
NME	*New Musical Express* magazine
NMN	nicotinamide mononucleotide
NMPKT	not many people know that
NMPR	not many people realize
NMR	nuclear magnetic resonance
NMS	never more so
NMSA	National Movers and Storage Association
NN	night-night
NNDO	neglect of nonbonded differential overlap
NNE	north-northeast
NNW	north-northwest
NO	nice one
No	number; know
NO1	no one

No1&0CnStopUNow
    no one and nothing can stop you now
NOL national outlook
Nome gnome
NoMreMr/MsNG
    no more Mr/Ms nice guy
NOn noon
NORSPA North Sea Special Programme of Action (EU)
NOW New Opportunities for Women (EU); New World Order
NOWI not only will I . . .
NowIsTRItTIm now is the right time
NOX nitrogen oxides
NOYB none of your business
NOYN not on your nelly!
NP no problem
N\P no problem
NPA Newspaper Publishing Association
NPC not politically correct
NPT Non-Proliferation Treaty
NPX numeric processor extension
NQA no questions asked
NQR nuclear quadruple resonance
Nrd nurd
NRN no reply/response necessary
NRPB National Radiation Protection Board
NS new style; Newspaper Society

NSF	National Schizophrenia Fellowship
NSN	never say no
NSNA	never say never again
NSPCC	National Society for the Prevention of Cruelty to Children.
NSPI	National Society of Performance and Instruction
NSS	National Secular Society
NSW	New South Wales
NT	New Testament; Northern Territory (Australia)
NT2NITE	not tonight
NTF	National Training Foundation
NTIBOA	not that I'm bitter or anything
NTIM	not that it matters
NtlS	nevertheless
NTSB	National Transportation Safety Board (US government)
NTTT	never trust the Tories
NUDAGO	National Union of Domestic Appliances and General Operatives
NUJ	National Union of Journalists
NULMW	National Union of Lock and Metal Workers
NUM	National Union of Mineworkers
NUMAST	National Union of Marine, Aviation and Shipping Transport Officers
NUPE	National Union of Public Employees (merged with others to form Unison)

NUT	National Union of Teachers
NV	Nevada (official postal abbreviation)
NV4M	not value for money
Nva	never
Nva2L8	never too late
NvaEtMorThnUCanLift	
	never eat more than you can lift
NvaGivUp	never give up
Nvamnd	never mind
NVC	nonverbal communication
NVQ	National Vocational Qualification
NW	nett weight; Net wars; northwestern; no worry/don't worry
NWNF	no win, no fee
Nxt	next
NxtD0r	next door
NY	New York (official postal abbreviation)
NYNY	New York, New York
NYP	not your problem
NZ	New Zealand

O

O	over (to you)
O!	oh!; over!
O!O!	Order! Order!
O2L	out to lunch
O2S	on to something
O2U	over to you
O4COL!	oh, for crying out loud!
O4GS!	oh, for goodness'/God's sake!
O4TC	out for the count
O&A	out and about
OAH	open all hours
OAO	on account of; old-age pension(er)
OAPEC	Organization of Arab Petroleum Exporting Countries
OAR	Open Architecture for Reasoning (EU)
OASC	open-and-shut case
OASIS	Open and Secure Information Systems (EU)
OAU	Organization of African Unity
OB	Order of the Bath; organizational behaviour; outside broadcast
OBE	Officer (of the Order of the) British Empire
OBO	or best offer
obsd	observed
OBTW	oh, by the way

OBTWIAU	oh, by the way, I adore you
Ocarm	Order of the Brothers of the Blessed Virgin Mary of Mount Carmel
Ocart	Order of Carthusians
OCR	optical character recognition/reader
OCT	Overseas Countries and Territories
OD	open debate; ordnance datum; organization development
ODA	online display of affection; Overseas Development Agency
ODAS	Ocean Data Acquisition System (EU)
ODBC	open database connectivity
ODBMS	object-oriented database management system
OECD	Organization for Economic Cooperation and Development
OED	*Oxford English Dictionary*
OEEC	Organization for European Economic Cooperation
OEM	original equipment manufacturer
OEXP	Office of Exploration (NASA)
OFM	often works for me
OFnsve	offensive
OFT	Office of Fair Trading
OFTC	out for the count
Ogr	ogre
OH	off hand; open house; Ohio (official postal abbreviation)

OHMS on Her/His Majesty's Service
OIC oh, I see
OIL options in law
OIN oh, it's nothing
OJ orange juice
OK OK/okay
OK Oklahoma (official postal abbreviation)
OL old lady (girlfriend, wife, mother); online; outlook
OL Open Learning
OLA online argument
OLAM or leave a message
OLATT online all the time
OLD online divorce
OLE object linking and embedding; Organizational Learning in Enterprises (EU)
OLEW Open Learning Experimental Workshop (EU)
OLL online love
OLM online marriage
OLR online relationship/romance
OLRow online row
OLS online split
OLTS Old Lady of Threadneedle Street (Bank of England)
OM old man (boyfriend, husband, father)
OM Order of Merit
OMD Outdoor Management Development

OMNI Overseas Moving Network Institute
On2 on to
ON4 on for
OnlETStrngSrvIv
 only the strong survive
OnlyU only you
OnlyU&Me only you and me
ONNA oh no, not again
o.n.o. or near offer
ONP Open Network Provision (EU)
ONUS on an unrelated subject
OO over and out
O&O over and over; over and out
OO2U options open to you
O&OA over and over again
OOB out of bounds
OOBE out-of-body experience
OODB object-oriented database
OOH out of hours
OOO out of order
OOSOOM out of sight, out of mind
OOT out of touch
OOTT out on the town/tiles
OOTW out of this world
OOTWX out-of-this-world experience
OP Order of Preachers
OPEC Organization of Petroleum-Exporting Countries

OPET	Organizations for the Promotion of Energy Technology (EU)
OPI	of paramount importance
OPnts!	oh, pants!
OpnUpYa<3	open up your heart
OpnUpYaMnd	open up your mind
OR	Oregon (official postal abbreviation)
ORD	optical rotatory dispersion
Org	organic; organize/organization
OS	old style; on something; operating system; ordinary seaman; Ordnance Survey; outsize
OSB	Order of St Benedict
OSCAR	Optical Switching Systems, Components and Architecture Research (EU)
OSIRIS	Optimal Standards for Successful Integration of Multimedia On-Line Services (EU)
OSIS	Open Shops for Information Systems (EU)
OSSAD	Office Support System Analysis and Design (EU)
OT	off topic; Old Testament
OT!	out there!
OTC	over-the-counter
OTEC	ocean thermal energy conversion
OTF	off the floor
OTH	on the hour
OTOH	on the other hand
OTS	off the shelf

OTSOTM	on the spur of the moment
OTT	on the train/tube; over the top
OTTOMH	off the top of my head
OTTtt!	way over the top!
OTW	off the wall; on the whole
OU	Open University
OUAT	once upon a time . . .
OUATITW	once upon a time in the west
OUP	Oxford University Press
OutStndn!	outstanding!
outta	out of (here)
OW	offworld(er); oh well
OW2TE	or words to that effect
OWMG	oh well, mustn't grumble
OWMM	one-worker/multiple-machines production
OWntUStAJstALTleBitLnga?	
	oh, won't you stay just a little bit longer
OWotAFElin	oh, what a feeling
OXFAM	Oxford Committee for Famine Relief
Oxon	Oxoniensis: of Oxford University
OYB!	on yer bike!
OYM	on your marks
OYMGSG!	on your marks, get set, go!
oz	ounce

P

P2G pretensions to grandeur
P3P Platform for Privacy Preferences Project
Pa pascal
PA Pennsylvania (official postal abbreviation); personal assistant; Press Association; public address
p.a. per annum
PAB personal address book
PABA para-aminobenzoic acid
PABX private automatic branch exchange (telephony)
PAC Pan-African Congress; political action committee
PACE Programme of Advanced Continuing Education (EU)
PAL phase alternation line
PAMELA Pricing and Monitoring Electronically of Automobiles (EU)
PANDORA Prototyping a Navigation Database of Road Network Attributes (EU)
PANGLOSS Parallel Architecture for Networking Gateways Linking Open Systems Interconnections (EU)
PANS pretty awesome new stuff (as opposed to POTS)

PAP	Prices and Agricultural Products (EU)
PARCMAN	Parking Management, Control and Information Systems (EU)
PAW	parents are watching
PAX	private automatic exchange (telephony)
PAYE	pay as you earn (taxation)
PBC	peripheral bus computer; processor bus controller
PBCD	packed binary-coded decimal
PBE	prompt by example
PBJ	peanut butter and jelly
Pbk	paperback
PBL	problem-based learning
PBRA	please be rest assured
PBS	public broadcasting service; public broadcasting system
PBT	profit before tax
PBX	private branch Exchange (telephony)
pc	parsec
PC	past caring; personal computer; phone card; Police Constable; politically correct; Poor Clares; Privy Councillor
P&CA	practical and constructive advice
PCB	please call back; polychlorinated biphenyls; printed circuit board
PCLI	independent political entity (republic)
PCM	please call me

PCMCIA people can't master computer industry acronyms; Personal Computer Memory Card International Association

PCP phenylcyclohexylpiperidine

PCS personal communication system; Public and Commercial Services Union

PctrThsUMeB%lesx2 picture this – you, me, bubble bath and champagne

pd paid

p.d. potential difference

PDA Packaging and Design Association, Europe; public display of affection

PDK polyester double knit

p.d.q. pretty damn quick

PDR precision depth recorder

PDS please don't shoot

PDT Pacific Daylight Saving Time

PE physical education

PEBCAK problem exists between chair and keyboard (it's the user's fault)

PEBrAn peabrain

PEI Prince Edward Island

PEN International Association of Poets, Playwrights, Editors, Essayists and Novelists

PeNEWIs£FOlish penny wise, pound foolish

PEP Political and Economic Planning; Personal Equity Plan
PERT programme evaluation and review technique
PET positron emission tomography; polyurethane terephthalate
PF Patriotic Front
PFA Professional Footballers' Association
PFC personal filing cabinet
PGA Professional Golfer's Association
PgDg pig dog
PGGB Pan-Galactic Gargle Blaster
PGP Pretty Good Privacy (encryption software)
Ph phenyl
PH Purple Heart
PHARE The Poland and Hungary Assistance for Economic Restructuring programme (EU)
PhD Doctor of Philosophy (Latin, *Philosopheae Doctor*)
PHIRM Profitable Human Investment and Resource Management
PHP personal homepage tool
phys physical(ly)
PIA Personal Investment Authority
PIBCAK problem is between chair and keyboard
PIMS personal information management system; profit impact of market strategy; Project on Integrated Management Systems (EU)

PIN	personal identification number
PIP	Priority Information Programme (EU)
PITA	pain in the arse/ass
PITB	pain in the bum/bottom/backside/butt
PITN	pain in the neck
PITP	pain in the posterior
PITR	pain in the rear/rear end
PJB	*Periodic Journal of Bibliography*
PK	psychokinesis
PklP$	picklepuss
PKU	phenylketonuria
PKZIP	shareware utility that allows users to compress data for storage and distribution
pl	place; plural
Pl8	plate
PLA	People's Liberation Army
PlA2Win	play to win
PLC	public limited company
PLCWTWU	Power Loom Carpet Weavers and Textile Workers Union
PLMKOK?	please let me know, OK?
Plnkr	plonker
PLO	Palestine Liberation Organization
PLS	please
PlsDntGo	please don't go
PM	postmortem; prime minister; private message
PM of F	Presidential Medal of Freedom

p.m.	post meridiem (afternoon)
PM4BR	pardon me for being rude
PM4BSRIWNMIWMFIJCU2SH&NIGBDB	
	pardon me for being rude, it was not me it was my food. It just came up to say hello, and now it's gone back down below.
PMFJIB	pardon me for jumping in but . . .
PMI	Pensions Management Institute
PMO	perturbational molecular orbital
PMP	practice makes perfect
PMP	laughing my arse off and peeing my pants
PMP	peeing my pants
PmpItUp	pump it up
PmpUpTVolUm	pump up the volume
PMWIBDMB	pardon me while I barf down my bra
PNDO	partial neglect of differential overlap
P & O	Peninsular and Oriental Steamship Company
POA	Prison Officers' Association
POB	place of birth
Pobl	possible
POD!	party on, dude!
PODA	Piloting of Office Document Architecture (EU)
POETSDAY	piss off early, tomorrow's Saturday
polymd	polymerized
polymg	polymerizing
polymn	polymerization

POM	peace of mind
POMM	piece of my mind
PONR	point of no return
::POOF::	goodbye (leaving the room)
POP3	Post Office Protocol 3
POPs	points of presence
POS	point of sale
PoS	possible
POSIX	portable operating system interface exchange (for computer environments)
POT	plain old telephone
POTS	plain old telephone service
POV	point of view
POW	prisoner of war
powd.	powdered
pp	pages
pp	*per pro.* (by proxy)
pp	pianissimo (very softly)
p&p	post and packing
PPA	Periodical Publishers Association
p.p.b.	parts per billion
PPI	plan position indicator
ppl	people
p.p.m.	parts per million
PPP	Pariser-Parr-Pople; point-to-point protocol
PPS	Parliamentary Private Secretary; additional postscript

ppsig	pounds per square inch gage
ppt	precipitate
pptd	precipitated
pptg	precipitating
pptn	precipitation
PR	please reply; proportional representation; public relations
PRA	Pre-Retirement Association
PRCA	Public Relations Consultants' Association
PRE	Pre-Retirement Education
PRECISE	Prospects for Extra-Mural and Clinical Information Systems Environment (EU)
PREDICT	Pollution Reduction by Information and Control Techniques (EU)
prep	prepare
prepd	prepared
prepg	preparing
prepn	preparation
PrfctDA	perfect day
PrfctWrld	perfect world
PrkFAc	prick face
PRO	Public Record Office; public relations officer
prodn	production
PROM	programmable read-only memory
PRP	performance/profit-related pay
PRs	mobile-phone races
PRS	pass (pron. as RP: 'pahs')

PRW	parents are watching
Prwn	prawn
PS	postscript; PlayStation
PSBR	public-sector borrowing requirement
psi	pounds per square inch
psia	pounds per square inch absolute
PST	Pacific Standard Time
PSV	public service vehicle
PSX	PlayStation (Sony's entertainment system)
PT	Pacific Time; physical training
pt	pint
PTA	parent–teacher association
PTB	pass the bucket; please text back
Pte	Private
PTFE	polytetrafluoroethylene (Teflon)
PTM	please text/tell me
PTO	please turn over
PTSB	pass the sick bucket
PTT	Pink Triangle Trust
PU!	that stinks!
PULSAR	Parking Urban Loading Unloading Standards and Rules (EU)
purifn	purification
PURMWyaMI	put your money where your mouth is
PUTP	pick up the pieces
PVA	polyvinyl acetate
PWA	Public Works Administration

Pwr	power
PWR	pressurized-water reactor
Pwr2TPEps	power to the people
PwrTxt	power text
PYaTIM	put your trust in me
PYO	pick your own
PZaFAc	pizzaface

Q

Q queue

QA quality assurance

QAMS Quality Assurance of Medical Standards (EU)

QANTAS Queensland and Northern Territory Aerial Services (Australia's national airline)

QARANC Queen Alexandra's Royal Army Nursing Corps

QB Queen's Bench

QBD quality by design (TQM principle)

QBE query by example

QBF query by form

QBI quite bloody impossible (RAF slang, said of flying conditions)

QC quality circle; quality control; Queen's Counsel

QCD quantum chromodynamics

QED quantum electrodynamics; quite easily done; quod erat demonstrandum (which was to be demonstrated)

QEF quod erat faciendum (which was to be done)

QF quick-firing

QI quartz-iodine

QiTWIIURAhed quit while you're ahead

QM Quartermaster

QMG Quartermaster-General
QMS Quartermaster-Sergeant
QNQ quantity not quality
QOL quality of life
QOS quality of service
QP queer politics
QPM Queen's Police Medal
qr quarter(s)
QSO quasar (quasi-stellar object)
QSS quasi-stellar radio source
QT cutie
qt quart(s)
q.t. (on the) quiet
qual qualitative(ly)
quant quantitative(ly)
QuEr queer
QUEST qualified employee share trust
q.v. which see (Latin, *quod vide*)
QWERTY standard keyboard (taken from top row of letters)

R

R are
R roentgen
R2KUp rushing to keep up
R4C request for comments
RA Rear-Admiral; Royal Academy; Royal Academician; Royal Artillery
RA rest assured
R&A Royal & Ancient Golf Club of St Andrews
RAAF Royal Australian Air Force
RAC Royal Automobile Club
RACE Research and Development in Advanced Communications Technologies in Europe
RADA Royal Academy of Dramatic Art
1FM Radio One (BBC)
RAeS Royal Aeronautical Society
RAF Royal Air Force
RAG red, amber, green
RAISE Rigorous Approaches to Industrial Software Engineering (EU)
RAM random-access memory; Royal Academy of Music
RAMC Royal Army Medical Corps
RAN Royal Australian Navy
RAOC Royal Army Ordnance Corps

RAOK	random act of kindness
RARTMB	round and round the mulberry bush
RASE	Royal Agricultural Society of England
RAT	relaxed attitude towards . . .
RB	ratbag
R&B	rhythm and blues; right button (of mouse)
RBBS	remote bulletin board system
RBC	red blood count
RBCS	Remote Bar Code System
RBS	Royal Bank of Scotland
RC	Roman Catholic
RCA	Royal College of Art
Rch4TSky	reach for the sky
Rch4T****	reach for the stars
RckMeBAB	rock me, baby
RCP	Royal College of Physicians
RCS	Royal College of Science; Royal College of Surgeons; Royal Corps of Signals
R&D	research and development
RDA	recommended daily allowance (dietetics)
RDAT	rotary-head digital audio tape
RDB	receive data buffer; relational database
RDBMS	relational database management system
RdMyLps-ILUVU	
	read my lips – I love you
RE	Royal Engineers
RECAP	Recycling of Automobile Plastics (EU)

RECITE	Regions and Cities in Europe
redn	reduction
ref	reference
REM	Radioactive Environmental Monitoring (EU); rapid eye movements
REMBASS	remotely monitored battlefield sensor system
REME	Royal Electrical and Mechanical Engineers
REMOBS	remote observation system
REMUS	Reference Models for Usability Specifications (EU)
reprodn	reproduction
RePTL	reptile
REQUEST	Reliability and Quality of European Software
resoln	resolution
resp	respective(ly)
ResQMe	rescue me
ResQOTW	rescue is on the way
RETAS	Retail Technology Plans (EU)
REWARD	Recycling of Waste Research and Development (EU)
REX	relocatable executable; remote execution
RF	radio frequency
RFD1	right from day one
RFTS	reach for the sky; right from the start
RFT***	reach for the stars
RFTWG	right from the word go
RGBI	red green blue intensity

rgds regards
RGS Royal Geographical Society
RHA Road Haulage Association
RHEED reflection high energy electron diffraction
RHF restricted Hartree-Fock
RI Rhode Island (official postal abbreviation)
RIAS Royal Incorporation of Architects in Scotland
RIBA Royal Institute of British Architects
RICS Royal Institute of Chartered Surveyors
RIE recognized professional body
RIMES Road Information and Management Eco-System (EU)
RINA Royal Institute of Naval Architects
RIP *requiescat in pace* (rest in peace)
RIPE RACE Integrity Primitive Evaluation (EU)
RIPs rest in pieces
RIR right is right
RIRWIW right is right, wrong is wrong
RISC reduced interaction set computer
RISTT respectfully, I say to thee
RItHreRItNow right here right now
RL real life (that is, when not chatting)
RLC right, left and centre
RLH raving/right little Hitler
Rlx relax
RM read me; Royal Marines
RMA Royal Military Academy

RMB	ring my bell
Rmba	remember
RmbaURA*	remember you are a star
RmbaYaMIn	remember you're mine
RMBR	remember
RML	read my lips
RMO	ring me on . . .
rms	root-mean-square
RMS	Royal Microscopical Society
RMT	National Union of Rail, Maritime and Transport Workers
RMTxtMsg	read my text message (*as in* read my lips)
RN	Royal Navy
RNA	ribonucleic acid; ring, no answer
RNase	ribonuclease
RNC	Royal College of Nursing
RNIB	Royal National Institute for the Blind
RNLI	Royal National Lifeboat Institution
ROB	remote order buffer
ROCB	rolling on the carpet barfing
ROCE	return on capital employed
ROF	rolling on the floor
ROFL	rolling on the floor laughing
ROFLMAO	rolling on floor laughing my arse/ass off
ROFLUTS	rolling on the floor unable to speak
ROFLWTIMiis	rolling on the floor with tears in my eyes
ROFWivU	rolling on the floor with you

ROH	Royal Opera House, Covent Garden
ROlTWrld	rule the world
ROM	read-only memory
ROP	right off planet
ROR	raffing out roud (Engrish for 'laughing out loud')
ROS	range of services
ROSAMES	Road Safety Management Expert System (EU)
ROSE	Research Open Systems Europe
RoSPA	Royal Society for the Prevention of Accidents
ROTBA	reality on the blink again
ROTF	rolling on the floor
ROTFL	rolling on the floor laughing
ROTFLABITC	rolling on the floor laughing and biting into the carpet
ROTFLHBO	rolling on the floor laughing his (her) butt off
ROTFLMAO	rolling on the floor laughing my arse off
ROTFLMAO&PMP	
	rolling on the floor laughing my arse off and peeing my pants
ROTFLMBO	rolling on the floor laughing my butt off
ROTFLMBOAPMP	
	rolling on the floor laughing my butt off and peeing my pants
ROTT	right over the top
ROTTFL	rolling on the floor laughing
ROYGBIV	red, orange, yellow, green, blue, indigo, violet

RP	received pronunciation
RPA	random phase approximation
RPC	Restrictive Practices Court
RPG	role-playing games
RPI	Retail Price Index
RPM	resale price maintenance
r.p.m.	revolutions per minute
Rpulsve	repulsive
RQ	respiratory quotient
R&R	round and round
R&R	rest and recreation
RRMTxtMsg	reread my text message
rRNA	ribosomal RNA
RS	Royal Society
RSA	Royal Society of Arts
RSC	Royal Shakespeare Company; Royal Society of Chemistry
RSH	Royal Society of Health
RSI	repetitive strain injury
RSM	Regimental Sergeant Major
RSN	real/really soon now
RSO	arsehole
RSPB	Royal Society for the Protection of Birds
RSPCA	Royal Society for the Prevention of Cruelty to Animals
RSS	Royal Statistical Society
RSVP	*répondez, s'il vous plaît* (please reply)

RSX	real-time resource sharing executive
RTBF	read the bloody FAQ
RTC	regional technology centre; round the clock
RTFM	read the fucking/f'n manual
RTG	radio-isotope thermoelectric generator

RThOsFEtYaOwnOrRUBrknThmIn4Aduk?

are those feet your own or are you breaking
them in for a duck

RTI	read the instructions
RTITB	Road Transport Industry Training Board
Rtn	return
RTPI	Royal Town Planning Institute
RTS	read the screen
RTS	request to send
RTWU	right there with you
RU	are you?
RUBRIC	Rule-Based Approach to Information Systems Development (EU)
RUF2T?	are you free to talk?
RUGAY?	are you gay?
RUOK?	are you OK?
RUOnMyWL?	are you on my wavelength?

RURdy2GOHmeNw?

are you ready to go home now?

RUReD2B<3Brkn?

are you ready to be heart broken?

RUReD2FlI	are you ready to fly

RUT?	are you there?
RUTM	rather you than me
RUU4I?	are you up for it?
RUUP4IT?	are you up for it?
RUYaS	right up your street
RUYRS	right up your street
RV	recreational vehicle; Revised Version (Bible)
RVO	Royal Victorian Order
RWF	right way forward
RWHFY?	are we having fun yet?
RWTS	rough with the smooth
RX	receive/receiver
RXD	Received Data
RY	are you . . . ?
RYA	Royal Yachting Association
RYO	roll your own (write your own program; derived from cigarettes rolled yourself with tobacco and paper)
RYTM	rather you than me

s	second
S	shall not/shan't; should not/shouldn't
S1EE	someone else entirely
S1VS	someone very special
S2E	strive/ing to ensure
S2gthaAATY	still together after all these years
S2S	side to side; so to speak
S2SM	stand to suffer most
S2US	speak to you soon
S3Z	smoke-free zone
S4L	Spam for life (what you may get when you become someone's customer or client
S8n	Satan
SA	Salvation Army; say; sex appeal; social airhead; Société Anonyme (French PLC); South Africa; South Australia; start again; straight-acting
SA	Sturm Abteilung (Storm Troopers)
SA+!	say yes
SABC	South African Broadcasting Corporation
SABENA	such a bad experience, never again
SABR	Society for American Baseball Research
SAC	Senior Aircraftman

SAD	seasonal affective disorder; Single Administrative Document (EU)
SaDO	saddo
Sadsak	sadsack
SAE/s.a.e.	stamped, addressed envelope
SAF	shopping and fucking
SAFE	Standard Authoring Facility Environment (EU)
SAIt&ILDoIt	say it and I'll do it
SAL	such a laugh
SALR	saturated adiabatic lapse rate
SALT	Strategic Arms Limitation Talks
SAM	surface-to-air missile
SAm2U	same to you
SAm2Uw/NobzOn	
	same to you with knobs on
Sapon	saponification
Sapond	saponified
Sapong	saponifying
SAREX	Shuttle Amateur Radio Experiment (NASA)
SARL	Société à Responsabilité Limitée (French private limited company)
SAS	Special Air Service; sticks and stones
SAST	Strategic Analysis in the Field of Science and Technology (EU)
SASWBMBBNCNHM	
	sticks and stones will break my bones but names cannot hurt me

SASWBMBBNWNHM
sticks and stones will break my bones but names will never hurt me

SAT scholastic aptitude test

SATB start at the beginning

S@TB start at the beginning

Satd saturated

SATDOC Satellite Mediated Controlled Experiment for Continuing Education and Monitoring Doctors (EU)

Satg saturating

Satn saturation

S@T** staring at the stars

SAVE Special Action Programme for Vigorous Energy Efficiency (EU)

SAYE save as you earn

SBC single-board computer

SBF single black female

SBH sequencing by hybridization

SBIG Santa Barbara Instrument Group (commercial supplier of astronomical instruments)

Sbk softback

SBR styrene butadiene rubber

SBS sick-building syndrome; Special Boat Service

SBT sad but true; screen-based telephone

SBU strategic business unit

SBWR simplified boiling-water reactor

SC South Carolina (official postal abbreviation)

s.c. subcutaneous(ly)

SC\GE she can't get enough

SCAUAATY still crazy about you after all these years

ScD Doctor of Science (Latin, *Scientiae Doctor*)

SCDI Scottish Council of Development and Industry

SCE saturated calomel electrode

SCENT System Customs Enforcement Network (EU)

SCF self-consistent field

SCGE she can't get enough

SCHMC Society of Catering and Hotel Management Consultants

Schm0 schmo

SCID severe combined immunodeficiency

SCIP Society of Competitor Intelligence Professionals (USA)

SCLC Southern Christian Leadership Conference

ScmBg scumbag

SCMT so-called modern technology

SCNR sorry, could not resist

SCP Society of Chiropodists and Podiatrists

ScrE scary

SC$ success

SCS! success!

SCSI small computer systems interface (pron. scuzzy)

SCUBA	self contained underwater breathing apparatus
SCX	specialized communications exchange
ScZBg	scuzzbag
ScZBL	scuzzball
SDB	safety deposit box
SDC	Society of Dyers and Colourists
SDC!	size does count!
SDDB	somewhat distributed database
SDI	selective dissemination of information; Strategic Defense Initiative (US)
SDK	software development kit
SDLP	Socialist Democratic and Labour Party
SDM!	size does matter!
SDP	Social Democratic Party
SDS	special drawing rights; Students for a Democratic Society
S&DS	specialized and dedicated service
SDU	Social Democratic Union
SE	southeastern; Scottish Enterprise
SEA	Single European Act
SEAQ	Stock Exchange Automated Quotation System
SEC	Securities and Exchange Commission
SECAM	Séquence Electronique Couleur avec Mémoir (Electronic Colour Sequence with Memory)
SEG	smeg-eating grin

SEM	scanning electron microscopy
SEms	seems
Sen	Senator; senior
SEN	State Enrolled Nurse
SEO	senior executive officer
SEP	somebody else's problem
sepd	separated
sepg	separating
sepn	separation
SEPON	Stock Exchange Pool Nominees
SERPS	State Earnings-Related Pension Scheme
SEsnsGrEtngs	seasons greetings
SETE	smiling ear to ear
SETI	Search for Extraterrestrial Intelligence
SEX	Software Exchange
SEXAFS	Surface Extended X-Ray Adsorption Fine Structure
sf	sforzando (with sudden emphasis – music)
SF	surfer-friendly (low-graphics website)
SFA	Securities and Futures Authority
SFM	sometimes/seldom/somehow works for me
SF/sci-fi	science fiction
Sft	soft
SFX	sound effects; special effects
SFX	special effects; sound effects
SG	stop, go
SGS	still going strong

Sgt	Sergeant
SH2SI	somebody had to say it
SHAEF	Supreme Headquarters, Allied Expeditionary Force
SHAPE	Supreme Headquarters, Allied Powers, Europe
SHCOON	shoot hot coffee out of nose
shd	should
SHF	super-high frequency
SHID	slaps head in disgust
ShIn	shine
SHInLIkA*	shine like a star
ShInOn	shine on
ShLICaLUOrNdgU4Bfst2moro?	shall I call you or nudge you for breakfast tomorrow?
Shrta$	shortass
ShtUp	shut up
SI	Système International
SIB	Securities and Investments Board
SIC	Standard Industrial Classification
SIESO	Society of Industrial Emergency Safety Officers
SII	Integrated Information Systems (EU)
SIMO	simultaneous motion (chart)
SINBAD	single income, no boyfriend, absolutely desperate (said mostly of females)

SIOP	Single Integrated Operation Plan
SIS	strength in specialization
SIT	stay in touch
SITAOME	she is the apple of my eye
SITD	still in the dark
SIYROB40	sleep in your own bed for once
SIz	size
SJ	Society of Jesus
SJAM8	she's just a mate
SK!	smoking kills!
Sk8	skate
Sk8r	skater
SkrwbL	screwball
SlAv2Luv	slave to love
SLBM	submarine-launched ballistic missile
SLCM	sea-launched cruise missile
SLDP	Social and Liberal Democratic Party (precursor to Lib Dems)
SLIP	serial line Internet protocol
SLR	self-loading rifle; single-lens reflex
SM	snail mail
S&M	slave & master (sadomasochism)
SMART	Small Firms Merit Aware for Research and Technology
SMEX	small explorers (space)
SmIlURButiful	smile, you are beautiful
SmL	small

SmLESox smelly socks

SMM8 she's my mate

SMMT Society of Motor Manufacturers and Traders

SMO serious mode on

SMOFF serious mode off

SmOkGtsInYaiis

    smoke gets in your eyes

SMS short messaging service

SMTP simple mail-transfer protocol

SN special needs

S&N stuff and nonsense

SNAFU situation normal, all fucked up

SNOBOL String Oriented Symbolic Language (programming language)

SNP Scottish National Party

SO sod off; significant other; spot on

SOA start over again; state-of-the-art

SOB son of a bitch

SOD sad old drunk

SOE Special Operations Executive

SoFa so far

SOHF sense of humour failure

SOHwAmIDoin? so . . . how am I doing?

SOInLuvWivU so in love with you

SOIPE set out in plain English

SOL smiling out loud; strictly off limits

soln solution

soly	solubility
SOM	state of mind
SOME1	someone
SOMY?	sick of me yet?
SONAR	sound navigation and ranging
SOOL	shit, out of luck
Soons	as soon as
SOOutaLuv	so out of love
SOpa*	superstar
SoR	Society of Radiographers
SORP	statements of recommended practice
SOS	Save Our Souls (help!) – international distress signal
SOS8N	spawn of satan
SOSImLstWchWA2YaPlAc?	
	help, I'm lost. Which way to your place?
SOT	sort of thing
SOTA	state-of-the-art
SOTO	so often take over
SOX	sound exchange
SP	starting price; stop preaching
S&P	salt and pepper
SPA	sound, practical advice
SPBSQSA	Society for the Preservation of Barbershop Quartet Singing in America
SPC	Society of Pension Consultants
SPE	Society of Petroleum Engineers

SPEBSQUA	Society for the Preservation and Encouragement of BarberShop Quartet Singing in America
sp. gr.	specific gravity
SPK2ME	speak to me
SPOA	Scottish Prison Officers' Association
SPQR	small profits and quick returns
SPS	Strategic Planning Society
SPTD	speak of the devil
sp vol	specific volume
sp wt	specific weight
sq	square
Sqn Ldr	Squadron Leader
SQUID	superconducting quantum interference device
SR	Socialist Revolutionaries
sr	steradian
SRA	Strategic Rail Authority
SRB	solid (fuel) rocket booster
SRE	sorry
SRESEms2BTHrdstWrd	
	sorry seems to be the hardest word
SRN	State Registered Nurse
SRO	self-regulatory organization
SRT	stay right there
SS	Saints; steamship; *Schutzstaffel* (Nazi Protection Squad); seriously sad

S&S	sticks and stones
SS&BF	ship shape and Bristol fashion
SSADM	Structured Systems Analysis and Design Method
SSE	south-southeast
SS><)))">	something smells fishy
SSI	small-scale integration
SSIA	subject says it all
SSL	secure socket layer
SSM	so sue me
SSR	Soviet Socialist Republic; Standard Statistical Region
SSSI	Site of Special Scientific Interest
Sstrs	sisters
SSW	south-southwest
St	Saint; street
ST	surf time
ST2MORO?	same time tomorrow?
STAATY	still together after all these years
StAnAliv	stayin' alive
STARLAB	Space Telecommunications and Radioscience Laboratory (Stanford University, CA)
START	Strategic Arms Reduction Talks
StAWivMeBAB	stay with me, baby
STB	set-top box; spot the ball
STBY	standby/stand by
StckOnU	stuck on you

STD	Sexually transmitted disease; spot the difference; subscriber trunk dialling
std	standard
StEd&MrsPEl	Steed and Mrs Peel
StEl	steel
STFW	search the fucking Web
Sth	something
SthLk	something like
StL	still
StLStndn	still standing
StndByYaMan	stand by your man
StndrdC	standard class
Stnkpot	stinkpot
StNNdMLLt	stunned mullet
STO	Slater-type orbital
STOL	short take-off and landing
StOl	stool
STR	short-term relationship
Str8DwnTLne	straight down the line
StrA	stray
StrngAsStEl	strong as steel
STrngEnuf	strong enough
StrtMOvn	start moving
ST:TNG	*Star Trek: The Next Generation*
STUD	shop until you drop
StUpd	stupid
STW	search the Web; smooth(ing) the way

STYD	shop until you drop
SU4M	stand up for me
Subj	subject
SUFID	screwing up face in disgust
SUIC	see you in court
Sum1	someone
SumTImSOn	some time soon
Sumwer	somewhere
SUN1IL2U	shut up, no one is listening to you
SurThng	sure thing
SUT	Society of Underwater Technology
SVGA	super-video graphics adapter
SvnALMyLuv4U	saving all my love for you
SvnGrce	saving grace
SVQ	Scottish Vocational Qualification
SW	software; southwestern
SW?	so what?; says who?; since when?
SWAG	stupid wild-arse guess
SWAK	sealed with a kiss
SWALK	sealed/sent with a loving kiss
SWAPO	South-West Africa People's Organization
SWAX	sealed with a kiss
SWDTL	somewhere down the line
SWDURTW?	since when did you rule the world
SwEtDrEmsRMAdOfThs	
	sweet dreams are made of this
SwEtDrms	sweet dreams

SwEtInspr8shn
              sweet inspiration
SwEtFrEdm! sweet freedom!
SwEtSmLOfSC$ sweet smell of success
SWG scientific wild guess
SWLXX sealed/sent with loving kisses
Swmpbrth swampbreath
SWNTL? so what's not to like?
SWOT strengths, weaknesses, opportunities, threats (business analysis tool)
SWR short-wave radio
SWS slow-wave sleep
SWSWU Sheffield Wool Shear Workers Union
SWXX sealed with kisses
SWYaP? so what's your problem
SWYP? so what's your problem
SX simplex signalling
SxA sex appeal
SXS step-by-step switching (telephony)
SXtrc Scalextric
sym. symmetric(al)(ly)

T

T2G	time to go
T2GGG	time to go, go, go
T2GX3	time to go, go, go
T2N	train to nowhere
T2SO	time to switch off
T3	trouble-free
T4A	together for always
T4AB	time for a break
T4ACB	time for a coffee break
T4ATB	time for a tea break
T4B	time for bed
T4LMK	thanks for letting me know
T4T	time for tea
T4TT	thanks for the thought
T8	(the) Tate
TA	Territorial Army
TA4N	that's all for now
TAB	Totalisator Agency Board
TAC	Total Allowable Catch (fisheries) (EU)
TACOE	terms and conditions of employment
TAF!	that's all, folks!
TAFN	that's all for now
TAH	take a hint
TAkIt2TLmt	take it to the limit

TAkItEzE	take it easy
TAkItHIr	take it higher
TAkYaTIm	take your time
Talisman	Transfer Accounting Lodgement for Investors (UK stock market)
TAM	television audience measurement
TANLAD	there ain't nothing like a dame
TANSTAAFL	there ain't no such thing as a free lunch
TAO	take/taking account of
TAPPI	Technical Association for Pulp and Paper Industry (USA)
TARDIS	Time and Relative Dimension in Space (sci-fi)
TARO	time's almost run out
TASS	Technical and Supervisory Section (of AUEW); Telegrafnoe Agentsvo Sovetskovo Soyuza (news agency)
TATW4NM	time and tide wait for no man
TAURUS	Transfer and Automated Registration of Uncertificated Stock
TAXI	transparent asynchronous transceiver interface
TB	terabyte (1,000 gigabytes); translation buffer; tuberculosis
T/B	Top and Bottom
TBA	to be activated; to be advised; to be announced; to be arranged; to be assigned
TBBH	to be brutally honest

TBC	to be continued/confirmed
Tbg	tea bag
TB/GDGOd	the boy/girl done good
TBH	to be honest
TBIsYTCum	the best is yet to come
TBL	the bottom line
TBM	tactical ballistic missile or (World War 2) torpedo bomber; tunnel-boring machine
TBO	time between overhaul
TBR	to be resolved
TBRS	the birds are singing
tbs	tablespoon
TBS	talk between ships
TBT	Technology Based Training
TBtchIsBak	the bitch is back
TBW	to be written
TC	take care; the sea; total commitment
T&C	terms and conditions
TCCB	Test and County Cricket Board
TCGE	they can't get enough
TCO	take control of
TCP/IP	transmission control protocol/Internet protocol
TCXO	temperature-controlled crystal oscillator
TD	Territorial Decoration
TD2U	totally devoted to you
TDcizunIsYas	the decision is yours

TDLB	Training and Development Lead Body
TDMA	time division multiple access
TDSS	time doesn't stand still
TDTU	totally devoted to you
TE	the end
TEAAT	the end and all that
TEAE-cellulose	triethylaminoethyl cellulose
TEC	Training and Enterprise Council
Tee	T-shirt
TEFL	teaching English as a foreign language
Tele	television
TELEX	teletypewriter exchange
TeLItLIkItIs	tell it like it is
temp	temperature
TESL	teaching English as a second language
TESOL	Teaching English to Speakers of Other Languages
TESSA	Tax-Exempt Special Savings Account
TEXT	YELLING
TFA	together for always
TFAB	time for a break
TFACB	time for a coffee break
TFATB	time for a tea break
TFB	time for bed
TFC	the final countdown
TFH	thread from hell (online discussion that just won't die)

TFrdgHldsNoTRrs4U

> the fridge holds no terrors for you

TFT time for tea

TG transgender

TGHAWFI the Greeks have a word for it

TGIF thank God it's Friday

TGInLuvWivU this girl's/guy's in love with you

TGNI the good news is

TGOdTBd&TUgly

> the good, the bad and the ugly

TGr8C take great care

TGWU Transport and General Workers' Union

ThAAntCEnOYt they aint seen nothing yet

thermodn thermodynamic(s)

TherRPlntEMre><)))">ITC

> there are plenty more fish in the sea

TherRPlntEMrePBlsOnTBEch

> there are plenty more pebbles on the beach

THF tetrahydrofuran

Thmslvs themselves

ThnkOfT££$$UVSAvd

> think of the money you've saved

ThnkThn think thin

THNQ thank you

ThrsAWrldOutSIdYaWndO

> there's a world outside your window

ThruTPwrOfIntenshunUATrctALTWelthUNEOrDslr
through the power of intention you attract all
the wealth you need or desire

ths this

Ths&Tht this and that

ThsAM this morning

ThsIsIt this is it

ThsIsTDA this is the day

ThsIsTRItTIm this is the right time

ThsIsYaLIf this is your life

ThsLTlePGE this little piggy . . .

ThsPM this afternoon

tht that

ThtDr$WldLOkGrtOnMyBdrOmFlr
that dress would look great on my bedroom
floor

ThtsAbFab that's absolutely fabulous

ThtsFntstc! that's fantastic

ThtSoKOl that's so cool

THX thanks

TI Textile Institute

TI2GO time to go

TIA Telecommunications Industry Association

TIA thanks in advance (used if you post a
question and are expecting a helpful reply)

TIADD2M this is all double-Dutch to me

TIAII tell it as it is

TIC	tongue in cheek
TIFF	tag image file format
TIFM	take it from me
TII	Transfer Technology Innovation and Industrial Information (Europe)
TiiHI	the ayes (I's) have it
TIm4Acshun	time for action
TIME	tears in my eyes
TINWIS	that is not what I said
TIOLI	take it or leave it
TIR	international road transport (French: Transport International Routier)
titrn	titration
TIY	that is why . . .
TJS	the January sales
TK	telekinesis
TkeAChnceOnMe?	
	take a chance on me?
TkeMyHndTkeMyHleLfe2CosICntSOSFLnInLuvWivU	
	take my hand, take my whole life, too, 'cos I can't help falling in love with you
TL	till/until
TLA	three-letter acronym
TLC	tender loving care
TLItsROnBtNo1IsHOm	
	the lights are on but no-one is home
TLK	talk

TLK2ME	talk to me
TLK2UL8R	talk to you later
TLK2YAL8R	talk to you later
TLK2YL8R	talk to you later
TLKn	talking
TLMeImDrmn	tell me I'm dreaming
TLMIMW	the law/lord moves in mysterious ways
TLNE	the list never ends
TLS	*Times Literary Supplement*
TlstTImISawLegsLIkThtTherWozAMSgTId210fThm	
	the last time I saw legs like that there was a message tied to one of them
T&M	time and motion
TM2F	tailor made to fit
TMA	Telephone Managers' Association; Theatrical Management Association
TMB	text me back
TMC	too many cooks
TMCSTB	too many chefs spoil the broth
TMI	too much information
TMINET	too much information, not enough time
TMIY	take me, I'm yours
TMO	text me on . . .
TMOL	the meaning of life
TMS	tailor-made solution
TMWBTC	that may well be the case
TN	Tennessee (official postal abbreviation)

TNA	Training Needs Analysis
TNN2S	there's no need to shout
TNO	the nature of
TNOTVS	there's nothing on TV, so . . .
TNT	trinitrotoluene
TO	time out; too
TOL	tub of lard
TOML	time of my life
TOnlEWAIsUp	the only way is up
TOnlyThngThtLOksGOdOnMeIsU	
	the only thing that looks good on me is you
TOPCA	till our paths cross again (early Celtic chat term)
TOPEX	Ocean Topography Experiment (TOPEX/POSEIDON is a joint US–French oceanography satellite)
TOrg	toerag
TOS	Tramiel Operating System
TOTBE	that's only to be expected
TOtl	total
TOTP	*Top of the Pops*
TOTP2	*Top of the Pops 2*
TOTT	totally over the top
TOU	thinking of you
TOY	thinking of you
TPONR	the point of no return
TPRE	the possibilities are endless

TpsyTrvy	topsy-turvy
TPTB	the powers that be
TPTP	the phrase that pays
TPwrIsYas	the power is yours
TQM	total quality management
TR14U	the right one for you
TRH	Their Royal Highnesses
TRIB	transfer rate of information bits
TRItTOl4Tjob	the right tool for the job
TrLL	troll
Trndoid	trendoid (trendy but robotic)
TRNN	the Richard Nixon rule
TrnUpTPwr	turn up the power
TRO	time's run/running out
TruLuv	true love
TS	time scale; transsexual; type script
TSB	Trustee Savings Bank
TSFF	that's so far-fetched
TSH	thyroid-stimulating hormone
TSIzURIBetUHavYaOwnPstCOd	
	the size you are, I bet you have your own post code
TSNE	the story never ends
TsooooU!	that's soooo unfair!
Tsp	teaspoon
TSS	typescripts
TSSA	Transport Salaried Staffs' Association

TT	the Tube; think tank; Tourist Trophy; tuberculin-tested; teetotal; teetotaller
T&T	trials and tribulations; tried and tested
TT4N	ta-ta for now
TTBE	that's to be expected
TTD	today's the day
TTEOAN	through the eye of a needle
TTFN	ta-ta for now
TTG	time to go
TTGGG	time to go, go, go
TTIAO	they think it's all over
TTImHsCum	the time has come
TTL	through the lens
ttl	total
TTL4N	that's the lot for now
ttlty	totality
ttly	totally
TTn	think-tanking
TTOML	the time of my life
TTOYaL	the time of your life
TTT	thought that, too (when someone types in what you were about to type)
TTTD	ten to the dozen
TTTS	too tired to shag
TTUL	talk to you later
T&TW4NM	time and tide wait for no man
TTYL8r	talk to you later

TU	thank you
TU4YaH	thank you for your help
TUA	Telecommunications Users' Association
TUC	Trades Union Congress
TULE	took you long enough
TUVLURWEL	thank you very little, you're welcome even less
TUVM	thank you very much
TV	television; transvestite
TVBOL	the very best of luck
TWB	The World Bank
TWDN	that will do nicely
TWE	time without end
TWhElsMvnBtTHmstrsDEd	
	the wheel's moving but the hamster's dead
TWI	Training Within Industry
TWIMC	to whom it may concern
TWIS	that's what I said
TWMA	till we meet again
TWTT	the worm that turned
TWUA*	to wish upon a star
TWUT	that's what you think
TX	Texas (official postal abbreviation); transmit/transmitter
Txt	text
Txt3Z	text-free zone
TxtLnd	Text Land

TxtMeBAB	text me, baby
TxtMsgRg	text-message rage
TxtOvrld	text overload
TxtSpEk	text speak
TYaL4N	that's your lot for now
TYVM	thank you very much
TZ	*The Twilight Zone*

U

U	you
U2D	up to date
U2MeREvrEThng	
	you to me are everything
U2TM	up to the minute
U2TS	up to the second
U2U	up to you
U4IT	up for it
U4Me	you for me
UAD	you always do
UAE	United Arab Emirates
UAN	up all night
U+Me=Luv	you plus me equals love
UAP	United Australia Party
UAPITA	you're a pain in the arse
UART	universal asynchronous receiver-transmitter
U@?	where are you?; where are you at?
UBlwMyMnd	you blow my mind
UBM<3	you break my heart
UBMH	you break my heart
UBR	Uniform Business Rate
UBrnFatEFrtlSlE	
	you burn fat effortlessly
UBS	you'll be sorry

UCAC	Undeb Cenedlaethol Athrawon Cymru (Welsh teachers' union)
UCAR	Union of Central African Republics
UCAROM	you can always rely on me
UCATT	Union of Construction, Allied Trades and Technicians
UCBS	you can't be serious
UCCL	you couldn't care less
UCDI!	you can do it
UCGE	you can't get enough

UCldGetAJobAsADcoy4AWAlinShp

you could get a job as a decoy for a whaling ship

UCldSwatFllsW/thseErs

you could swat flies with those ears

UCLIU	you can look it up
UCLOM	you can lean on me
UCMI	you can make it

UcnDoItIfUOnlEThnkUCan

you can do it if you only think you can

UCnDoMgic	you can do magic

UCnGtItIfURELEWan

you can get it if you really want

UCnHavItAL	you can have it all

UCnNevaB2RichOr2Thn

you can never be too rich or too thin

UCSFTT	you can't say fairer than that

U&D up and down
UDA Ulster Defence Association
UDB unified database
UDI Unilateral Declaration of Independence
UDM Union of Democratic Mineworkers
UDntHav2SAULuvMe
you don't have to say you love me
UDntNoTMninOfTWrdFearInFctUDntNoTMninOfALotOfWrds
you don't know the meaning of the word
fear; in fact you don't know the meaning of a
lot of words
UDO under doctor's orders
UDontNEdOInsted
you don't need anything to replace cigarettes
UDoSumthng2Me
you do something to me
UDR Ulster Defence Regiment
UDsrveSCe$ you deserve success
UEFA Union of European Football Associations
UFascin8Me you fascinate me
UFLT you frisky little thing
UFO unidentified flying object
UFVU you frisky vixen, you
UGetWUxpctNtWUDsrvXpctTBEST
you get what you expect, not what you
deserve – expect the best
UglE ugly

UGoTaBlEv	you gotta believe
UGotIt	you got it
UGotSOl	you got soul
UGotTPwr	you've got the power
UGtTPwr	you've got the power
UGtWotItTAks	you've got what it takes
UH2BT	you had to be there
UHavARIt2BfrE	you have a right to be free
UHavARIt2Bluvd	
	you have a right to be loved
UHavFAthInYaSlf	
	you have faith in yourself
UHBW	you have been warned
UHF	ultra-high frequency
UHL	you have lost
UHT	ultra-high temperature
UILI	Union Internationale des Laboratoires Independants UK
UKASCII	variant of ASCII that takes account of some British key conventions
UKELA	UK Environmental Law Association
UKWIM	you know what I mean
UKWUCD	you know what you can do
UL@@KDITD	you look down in the dumps
ULD	you'll do
ULDITD	you look down in the dumps
ULItMyFre	you light my fire

ULOkGr8&FElGr8
> you look great and feel great

ULOkLIk$1MALGrEn&RinklE
> you look like a million dollars – all green and wrinkly

ULOkTRFicInASwmsuit
> you look terrific in a swimsuit

ULU University of London (students') Union

UMA union membership agreement

U&Me you and me

UMHXRayii you must have X-ray eyes

UMI you made it

UMMV your mileage may vary (you may not have the same luck I did)

UN United Nations

UNABOMBER university (and) airline bomber (Theodore Kaczynski, who was sentenced to life for a 17-year bombing campaign in the USA)

UNCTAD United Nations Conference on Trade and Development

UND you never do/did

UNDC United Nations Disarmament Commission

UNDP United Nations Development Programme

UNEP United Nations Environment Programme

UNESCO United Nations Economic, Scientific and Cultural Organization

UNFAO	United Nations Food and Agriculture Organization
UNFDAC	United Nations Fund for Drug Abuse Control
UNGA	United Nations General Assembly
UNHCR	United Nations High Commission for Refugees
UNHRC	United Nations Human Rights Commission
UNICEF	United Nations International Children's Emergency Fund
UNIDO	United Nations Industrial Development Organization
UNM	under new management
UNNF	you need never feel . . .
UNO	United Nations Organization
UNoWotUCnDo	you know what you can do
UNRWA	United Nations Relief and Works Agency for Palestine Refugees in the Near East
UNSG	United Nations Secretary General
UNTT	United Nations Trust Territory
UOH2A	you only have to ask
UP	Unwired Planet
Up2	up to
Up2Scrtch	up to scratch
Up2U	up to you
UPS	uninterruptible power supply; UV photoelectron spectroscopy
UPU	Universal Postal Union

UR under review; you are; your

UR1SndwchShrtOfAPiKnk

> you are one sandwich short of a picnic

URA you are affectionate

URAFction8 you are affectionate

URAFInanshal-=#:-)

> you are a financial wizard

URAGD you are a gold digger

URALEnMEnMchEn

> you are a lean mean machine

URAL<3 you are all heart

URAnACdntWAtn2HPn

> you are an accident waiting to happen

URAnInspir8shun

> you are an inspiration

URAsMchUsAsMdGrdsOnATortus

> you are as much use as mudguards on a
> tortoise

URA*NActLIk1 you are a star, now act like one

URAsUsfLAsAChocl8Tpot

> you are as useful as a chocolate teapot

URATA you are a tight arse

URBtifl you are beautiful

URCalm&:-)) you are calm and cheerful

URDMM you're driving me mad

URFleSBrAv&Bold

> you are fearless, brave and bold

URGR8	you are great
URGr8nOnMyNrvs	
	you are grating on my nerves
URGrgus	you are gorgeous
URGTnBeTa&BeTa	
	you are getting better and better
URL	universal (or uniform) resource locator
URL8D	you're late, dude
URLI	you're losing it
URLIkTVnusDMIloVBtiflBtNotALTher	
	you are like the Venus de Milo – very beautiful but not all there
URLoco!	you are crazy/mad
URLuv	you are love
URMNO1	you're my number one
URN	you are not
URNE2UT	you are not expected to understand this?
URNtAlOn	you are not alone
UROl!	you rule!
UROnMyWL	you are on my wavelength
UROYaO	you're on your own
URR	urgent reply required
URS	you arse
URS4EVA	yours sincerely for ever
URSchA*	you are such a star
URSF	yours faithfully

URSoMEnTQunBlnksWenUOpnYaWaLT

you are so mean the Queen blinks when you open your wallet

URSOOldUCnRmbaWenMdmeBuTrFlyWasOnlyACatrpLa

you are so old you can remember when Madame Butterfly was only a caterpillar

URSOOldUCnRmbaWenMoBDikWozOnlyATdPOl

you are so old you can remember when Moby Dick was only a tadpole

URSOOldUCnRmbaWenTDedCWasJstIL

you are so old you can remember when the Dead Sea was only ill

URSOShrtIfUPuLdUpYrSoxUdBBlndfld

you are so short that if you pulled up your socks you would be blindfold

URSS yours sincerely

URT you are tight

URT1 you are the one

URT4CBhndTPwr

you are the force behind the power

URTAOME you are the apple of my eye

URTBstThngThtsEvaHPnd2Me

you're the best thing that's ever happened to me

URTGr8st you are the greatest

URTTops you are the tops

URUDO you're under doctor's orders

URVW	you're very welcome
URVWIA	you're very welcome in advance
URW	you're welcome
URWIA	you're welcome in advance
URWlcm	you're welcome
URWrm&Luvabl	you are warm and lovable
URX:-"	you are an ex heavy smoker
URX:-Q	you are an ex smoker
USAF	United States Air Force
USB	universal serial bus
USBM	United States Bureau of Mines
USCG	United States Coast Guard
USCGAUX	United States Coast Guard Auxiliary
USD	upside down
USDAW	Union of Shop, Distributive and Allied Workers
USENET	users' network – bulletin boards on the Internet
USIS	United States Information Service
USM	unlimited securities market
USP	unique selling proposition/point; United States Pharmacopoeia
USSR	Union of Soviet Socialist Republics
UT	Utah (official postal abbreviation)
UTA	Unit Trust Association
UTC	under the circumstances
UTLKIN2ME?	you talking to me?

UTMeREvrEthng
> you to me are everything

UTW Union of Textile Workers

UUDO you're under doctor's orders

UV ultraviolet; you've

UV-B ultraviolet (radiation) B

Uve you've

UVG2BK you've got to be kidding

UvGotAFAcLIkASqEzdTBag
> you've got a face like a squeezed tea bag

UvGotANIcPrOfLgsSpeciallyTLft1
> you have got a nice pair of legs especially the left one

UvGotasMchClaSAsTrnWLPApa
> you've got as much class as torn wallpaper

UvGotMreChnsThnAChInEsFOnBOk
> you've got more chins than a Chinese phone book

UW you're welcome

UWFM usually works for me

UWnAgn you win again

UWST you'll show them

UWUWUWUWUWUWUW
> you will, you will, you will, you will, you will, you will, you will

UWWI you will walk it

UXB unexploded bomb

UXD unexploded device
UXM unexploded mine
UXO unexploded ordnance

V

V   volt
V4M   value for money
VA   Veterans Administration
VA   Virginia (official postal abbreviation)
V&A   Victoria and Albert Museum
VAT   value-added tax
VB   variable block; venture business
VBA   Visual Basic for Applications (Microsoft)
VBBS   virtual backbone service (a network backbone layered on another network)
VBE   VESA Bios Extender
VBG   very big grin
VBI   vertical blanking interval (portion of video signal used to transmit data)
VBR   variable bit rate
VBSEG   very big smeg-eating grin
VBV   video buffer verifier
VC   Victoria Cross
VCR   video cassette recorder
VD   venereal disease; Volunteer Decoration
VDU   visual display unit
VeGe   veggie (vegetarian)
VGA   video graphics adapter
VH   virtual hug

VHF	very high frequency
VHS	Video Home Service
VIBA	virtual-instruction-buffer address
VIP	vasoactive intestinal polypeptide; very important person
VK	virtual kiss
VLDB	very large database
VLF	very low frequency
VLSI	very large-scale interpretation
VM	voicemail
VMS	vertical marketing system
VOA	Voice of America
vol	volume
VOX	voice-operated transfer (to switch from receiving to transmitting)
VPM	very private message
VR	virtual reality
VRD	Royal Naval Volunteer Reserve Officers' Decoration
VRML	virtual-reality modelling language
vs/v	versus
VSO	Voluntary Service Overseas
VT	Vermont (official postal abbreviation)
VTOL	vertical take-off and landing
VTR	video tape recorder
vv	verses; volumes
VVCAMCS?	voulez-vous couchez avec moi ce soir?

VWB Visual Workbench (Microsoft)
Vxn vixen

W

W	watt
W/	with
W	will not/won't; without; would not/wouldn't
W1WF	witless one-word follow-up
W2B4	what to budget for
W3C	World Wide Web Consortium
W4M	wait for me; works for me
W4MT	wait for me there
W8	wait
W84Me@	wait for me at . . .
W8n	waiting
WA	Washington (official postal abbreviation)
WA2	well able to . . .
WAAC	Women's Auxiliary Army Corps
WAAF	Women's Auxiliary Air Force
WABI	Windows Application Binary Interface
WAC	Women's Army Corps
Wadya	what do you . . .?
WAEF	when all else fails
WAIS	wide-area information savers/search
Wak0	whacko
WALOOR	what a load of old rubbish
WAN	wide-area network

WAN2	want to
WAN2TLK?	want to talk?
WANA	we are not amused
WAP	wireless application protocol
WAPOR	World Association of Public Opinion Researchers
WAQuErDo	what a queer do
WASP	White Anglo-Saxon Protestant
WAV	wave-form audio – Windows standard for storing audio
WAWTG!	what a way to go!
WB	Warner Bros; water ballast; World Bank
WB	welcome back
WBA	World Boxing Association
WBC	white blood cells; World Boxing Council
WBL	Web-based learning; work-based learning
WBM	Web-based management
WBMP	Wireless Bitmap (is the default picture format for WAP)
WBO	with bells on
WC	water closet; West Central
WCB	will call back
WCC	World Council of Churches
W/Cdr	Wing Commander
WCL	World Confederation of Labour
WD	wet dream
wd	would

W&D	warehouse and distribution
WDA	Welsh Development Agency
WDALYIC?	who died and left you in charge?
WDHTHLL?	what does he think he looks like?
WDs	wet dreams
WdSht!	weird shit!
WDSTSLL?	what does she think she looks like?
WDTTTLL?	what do they think they look like?
WDU?	why don't you . . .?
WD\U?	why don't you . . . ?
WDUMBT?	what do/did you mean by that?
WDWWH2	we did what we had to
WDYAP	well do ya, punk?
We@	we are at . . .
WEA	Workers' Education Association
WEBCAM	Web camera
WebP	Web phone
w.e.f.	with effect from
WenCnICUAgn?	when can I see you again?
WenEvrULOkUpTherShLIB	
	whenever you look up there shall I be
WenILOkIntoYaiisICnCNo1isDrIvin	
	when I look into your eye I can see no one is driving
WenURLarfnTHOlWrldLarfsw/U	
	when you're laughing the whole world laughs with you

WeR@	we are at . . .
WerRU?	where are you?
Werv u bin?	where have you been?
WEST	Western Europe Summer Time
WET	Western Europe Time
WF	wallflower; Web favourite
WFM	works for me
WFTU	World Federation of Trade Unions
W\G	without guilt
WGC	World Gold Council
WGGB	Writers' Guild of Great Britain
WGRT	with greatest respect(s) to
WGT?	who goes there
WHAGOT	we/we've had a gay old time
WHO	World Health Organization
whr	where
WhrRU@?	where are you at?
WhrRUNow?	where are you now?
WhrTNow?	where are they now?
WI	(National Federation of) Women's Institutes; Women's Institute
WI	Wisconsin (official postal abbreviation)
WIAN?	what's in a name?
WIBNI	wouldn't it be nice if . . .
WICIWIW	what I see is what I want
WILG2TFOOAS	well, I'll go to the foot of our Auntie's stairs

WIMP	Windows, icons, mouse pointer (standard term to describe a system employing these)
WIPO	World Intellectual Property Organization
WIR	when in Rome
WISIWIW	what I see is what I want
WISRR!	when I say run . . . run!
WIST	wish I'd said that
WIT	Women in Training
WIT?	what is that?
WITM?	what is the matter?
WITOT	wish I'd thought of that
WITT	we're in this together
Wiv	with
Wiv	without
Wivin	within
Wivout	without
WIW	wrong is wrong
Wk	week
Wkly	weekly
Wknd	weekend
Wkndr	weekender
Wkndrs	weekenders
Wknds	weekends
WL	wavelength
Wlcm	welcome
WLDne!	well done

WldULIkSum12GoWivYaDrnk?
would you like someone to go with your drink?

WldULIkTPlsrOfMyCo?
would you like the pleasure of my company

WLGoTaDw/I what's luck got to do with it

WlkOnAr walk on air

WlkOnSnShIn walk on sunshine

WLSpk2UL8r will speak to you later

WLUBAB who loves you baby

WLUMREMe? will you marry me?

WLUStLLuvMe2moro?
will you still love me tomorrow?

WLWTCDI well, look who the cat dragged in

WMGRT with my greatest respect(s) to

WML wireless markup language

WMLScript wireless markup language script

WMO World Meteorological Organization

Wmp wimp

WMRT with my respect(s) to

Wnk wank

Wnkr wanker

WNO Welsh National Opera

W/o without

WOA work of art

WOG without guilt

WOLOGOMBA	without loss of generality, one may be assured (that . . .)
WOM	word of mouth
WORM	write once, read many
WOT	waste of time
Wot?	what?
WotCnIDo2MAkUMIn?	
	what can I do to make you mine?
WOTT	way over the top
Woublt	would you be able to . . . ?
WP	whoever/whenever/wherever/whatever/whichever possible; word processor/processing
WPA	Work Projects Administration
WPC	Woman Police Constable
WPD	word-processed document
w.p.m.	words per minute
WR2	with respect to
WRAC	Women's Royal Army Corps
WRAF	Women's Royal Air Force
wrd	word
WrdprcSr	word processor
Wrk	work
WrkBOK	work book
Wrkout	workout
WrkOvr	work over
WrkThtMagc	work that magic

WRNS Women's Royal Naval Service
WRS work-related stress
WRT with respect(s) to
WRULOkn@4ii?
what are you looking at, four-eyes?
WRVS Women's Royal Voluntary Service
WS web store
WS website
WSHC website health check
Wshn&Hpn&Thnkn&Prayn
wishing and hoping and thinking and praying
WSLS win some, lose some
WSP wireless session protocol
WST Western Standard Time
WSTD! well, shut that door!
wt weight
WT? what/who the?
WT? what's that?
Wt4MeDrln wait for me, darling
WTA wireless telephony application
WTAI wireless telephony application interface
WTB wanted to buy
WTC what the cruk?
WTCH what the crukking hell?
WTF what the fuck?
WTF!O! what the fuck! Over!
WTFH what the fucking hell?

WTG!	way to go!
WTGP?	want to go private?
WTH	want to help?; what/who the heck; what the hell?
WTLS	Wireless Transport Layer Security
WTM?	what's the matter?
WTO	World Trade Organization
WTOS	with the opposite sex
WTSS	with the same sex
WTTW	word to the wise
WU?	what's up?
WUBS?	will you be sad?
WUBT?	will you be told?
WUCBWH	wish you could be here
WUCIO?	will you cut it out?
WUCIWUG	what you see is what you get
WUET?	will you phone home?
WUF?	where are you from?
WUJL?	will you just listen?
WUJSUAL?	will you just shut up and listen?
WUMM?	will you marry me?
WUPH?	will you phone home?
W\USASO	wouldn't you say so?
WUWH	wish you were here
WV	West Virginia (official postal abbreviation)
WVA	well-versed argument
WVS	Women's Voluntary Service

WW	worldly wise
WW1/WWI	World War One
WW2/WWII	World War Two
WWF	World Wide Fund for Nature
WWM	*Watch With Mother*
WWOTT	way, way over the top
WWW	World Wide Web
WWW	World Wide Web; Why? Why? Why?
WWWHT	well, who would have thought
WWWOTT	way, way, way over the top
WY	Wyoming (official postal abbreviation)
WYaP?	what's your point?
WYaSOH?	where's your sense of humour
WYSBYGI	what you see before you get it
WYSIWYG	what you see is what you get

X

X	kiss
XC	Xerox copy (being sent to individual or organization name that follows)
XCF	experimental computing facility
xclusv	exclusive
xclusvly	exclusively
XclusvlyYRS	exclusively yours
XCOPY	extended copy
XcusMe?	excuse me?
XcusMeCnUGivMeDrctns2Ya<3?	excuse me, can you give me directions to your heart?
XDS	Xerox Data Systems (computer division of Xerox corp.)
XF	X File
XFER	Transfer
XIOS	extended input/output system
XL	extra large
XLAT	translate
Xlnt	excellent
XLnt	excellent
XMA	kiss my arse
XMe	kiss me
XMeQk	kiss me quick

XMeSlwly kiss me slowly
XMIT transmit
XML extensible markup language
XMRS kiss my arse
XMTR transmitter
XO executive officer
XOFF transmitter off
XON transmitter on
XOR exclusive or (logical function)
XOTC kiss on the cheek
XOTL kiss on the lips
Xoxoxoxo hugs and kisses
XP Jesus Christ (from the first two letters of 'Christ' written in Greek)
XPDR transponder
XPM XPixMap
XPORT transport
XPS X-ray photoelectron spectroscopy
XPS X-ray-induced photoelectron spectroscopy
XRC extended remote copy
XRD X-ray diffraction
XREF cross-reference
XRF X-ray fluorescence
XTP Express Transfer Protocol
Xtreme extreme
Xtrmnte exterminate
XUV extreme ultraviolet (space)

XVGA extended video graphics array (graphic mode)

Xxx kisses

XYZ examine your zip/zipper

XYZPDQ examine your zipper pretty darn quick

Y

Y2MeREvrEthng you to me are everything

YA yet another

Ya your

YABA yet another bloody acronym

YaBestISGOdEnuf

your best IS good enough

YaBrthIsSwEt&YaLngsRClr

your breath is sweet and your lungs are clear

YaBumLOksBigInTht

your bum looks big in that

YaConfdnceShwsOnYaFAc

your confidence shows on your face

YaFEtRSoBigUCldStmpOutBushFIrs

your feet are so big you could stamp out
forest fires

YaFOC you're full of clichés

YaFOS you're full of shit

YaiisRLIkPOls – MuDyPOls

your eyes are like pools – muddy pools

YaLiftDsntREchTTopFlOr

your lift doesn't reach the top floor

YaMemresSoBadYaMamaUsed2rapYaLnchInARdMap

your memory's so bad your mother used to
wrap your lunch in a road map

YAPITA	you're a pain in the arse
YaShpIsCumnIn	
	your ship is coming in
Yaslf	yourself
YaTEthRLIkT**sThyCumOut@NIt	
	your teeth are like the stars, they come out at night
YaTImHsCum	your time has come
YB	yearbook
YBMH	you break my heart
YBS	you'll be sorry
YCCL	you couldn't care less
YCGE	you can't get enough
YC\GE	you can't get enough
yd	yard
YdLOd	wide load
YD\U?	why don't you . . . ?
YFLT	you frisky little thing
YFVY	you frisky vixen, you
YG	young gentleman
YGBSM	you gotta be shittin' me
YGBSM	you gotta be shitting (sh't'n) me!
YHA	Youth Hostels Association
YHM	you have mail
YKWYCD	you know what you can do
YL	young lady
YL@@KDITD	you look down in the dumps

YLD	you'll do
YLDITD	you look down in the dumps
YM	young man
YMCA	Young Men's Christian Association
YMHA	Young Men's Hebrew Association
YMMV	your mileage may vary (you may not have the same luck I did)
YMNO1	you're my number one
YN?	why not?; why now?
YngFrE&Sngl	young free and single
YOB	year of birth
YOYO	you're on your own
YPEPuP	yuppie puppy (new rich kid)
yr	year; your
YRDMM	you're driving me mad
YRGR8	you are great
YRL8D	you're late, dude
yrly	yearly
YRM	your move
YROnMyWL	you are on my wavelength
yrs	years
YRS	you arse
YRS4Eva	yours sincerely
YRSF	yours faithfully
YRSS	yours sincerely
YRT	you are tight
YRTAOME	you are the apple of my eye

YRUDO	you're under doctors orders
YT	youth training
YTLKINTME?	you talking to me?
YUDO	you're under doctor's orders
YUPPIE	Young Urban (or Upwardly mobile) Professional (person)
YVW	you're very welcome
YVWIA	you're very welcome in advance
YW	you're welcome; young woman
YWCA	Young Women's Christian Association
YWHA	Young Women's Hebrew Association
YWIA	you're welcome in advance
YYSSW	yeah, yeah, sure, sure, whatever

Z

ZDO zero differential overlap
ZETA zero energy thermonuclear assembly
ZEV zero emissions vehicle
ZG zero gravity
Zng!WntTStrngsOfMy<3
  zing! went the strings of my heart
Zt zit (spot)
ZTFAc zitface
Zzzz I'm bored/boring; I'm tired

EMOTICONS

-!-!-!	NO! NO! NO!
'!	grim
-!	no
-!!	definitely not
!-(	I'd like to thank whoever gave you that black eye
!¬(	a black eye
""	sour puss
-"	whistling casually
#:-)	smiling with a fur hat
#:-0	oh, no!
$	double S
%	double B
%-)	cross-eyed; I am drunk but happy
%*@:-(	I am hung over with a headache
%-}	intoxicated
%+{	you are a loser
%-<I>	I am drunk with laughter (not)
%-6	not very clever
&:-)	smiling with curls
&:-]	you are very handsome with square jaw
(: -)	URClvr! good luck in your exams
(:+(	ooh I'm scared
((_0_))	fat arse

((H)))	a big hug
(-)	get your hair cut
('.')	a dog
(-.-)ZZzz	a dog asleep
(-:	also smiling; smiling back; I am left-handed
(:-&	angry
(:-)	shame you lost the last hair; smiling with helmet
(:-{~	the beard really suits you
(:-|K-	this is a formal message
(:-...	I am heart-broken
(:-D	blabber mouth
(@ @)	you're kidding!
(]:-)	I am gung ho
(^o^)	I am joyously singing your praises
(-_-)	this is my secret smile (sideways)
(_„_)	fat arse
(_?_)	dumb arse
(_o_)	an arse that's been around
(_0_)	an arse that's been around even more
(_x_)	kiss my arse
(><)	you are anally retentive
(c:	bloke/bunny with big nose
(C:	smiling big nosed bloke
('o')=***	a dog barking
(0—<	fishface
)|-[	you are tired, grumpy and very sad

)i({	butterfly
*	star
!#!^*&:-) ?	schizophrenic? I don't like either of you
**	stars
**-(	I am very, very shocked
:/I	well done you've stopped smoking!
**ITE	stars in their eyes
*:-o	someone who is really scared
*:0)	bozo
*^_^*	a huge dazzling grin
*<8-)X	why don't you wear your fantastic new party outfit with hat and bow-tie
B	blink
G	giggle or grin
H	hug
L	I am blotto (sideways)
S	sob
W	wink
X	kiss
.^,	I am looking sideways/happy
.0+I)=:	a ballerina
.0+I)=::	a ballerina standing tip toes
-/-	you are a stirrer
/0\	I am ducking
:-(	sad
:-)	happy
:-))	cheerful

:-)))**Xmas** happy Christmas

: (:) you pig!

:') happy and crying

:-) **&LOkEmInT iis**

smile and look 'em in the eyes

:-))) very happy

:-)))**ANvrsrE** happy anniversary

:-)))**BrthdA** happy birthday

:@ shouting

:t pouting

:! foot in mouth

:-" heavy smoker

:-# my lips are still sealed

:#) I am drunk every night

:-#| I love the bushy moustache

:-$ put your money where your mouth is

:-% merchant banker

:-& I feel tongue-tied

:-(boo hoo

:'-(crying; I am crying

:-(sad

:(sad, without nose

:-() shocked; smiling with mouth open

:-(**YaBrAnIsntAsBgAsYa (_,,_)**

what a pity your brain isn't as big as your bottom

:-0 give me a snog

:-(*)	that comment made me sick
:(*)	you make me sick
:-(~~	I'm sick; I've been sick
:-(0)	shouting
:-)—	98-pound weakling
:-)	ha ha
:)	happy
:'-)	I am so happy, I am crying
:-)	I'm joking
-:-)	punk
:-)'	shall I get you a bib?
:-)	smiling
:)	smiling without a nose
:————————)	
	you are a big liar; Pinocchio
:-)*<|-)	happy Christmas
:):):)	loud guffaw
:)))	hugging that beer belly is like waking up holding a cold hot water bottle
:-)))	reeeaaaalllly happy
:-)))?	how many chins is it now?
:-)}	. . . and the goatee
:-)~	I am drooling (in anticipation)
:-)=	goofy; smiling with a beard
:-)8	smiling with bow tie; you look great
:-)K-	a shirt and tie at the gym – please?
:-*	bitter; bitter, moi?; kiss; ooops!

:-**	kisses
:*(	I am crying softly
:*(@)	you are drunk and shouting
:*)	I am drunk
:*)?	are you drunk?
:-/	I am sceptical
!-(	black eye
!:-)	imaginative
#-)	partied all night
#:-)	bad hair day
#:-@	frightened
#:-]	harassed/bad hair day
#8^0-|-<	full-bodied
$(:-|	soldier
$-)	yuppie
$:-$	stockbroker
$:-)	comb stuck in the hair
$:-) : 8-	gigolo
$__$	sees money
%-$	hangover
%-(	broken glasses
%-(|)	laughing out loud
%-)	drunk grin
%\v	Pablo Picasso
%-{ :/)	not amused
%-|	been working all night
%-}	amused

%')	very drunk
&.(..	crying
&-|	tearful/that made me cry
(:+(	scared
((((name))))	hug
(()):**	hugs and kisses
()	feeling in harmony; connecting
(-)	needing a haircut
())=(	wine glass
(-:	an Australian; left-handed
(: (=|	ghost costume
(:-#	said something stupid
(:-$	ill
(:-& :-||	angry
(-::-)	putting heads together
(::[]::)	Band-aid; offering help or support
(-:|:-)	Siamese twins
(:+)	big nose
(:=)	long nose
(:>-<	hands up – I quit/surrender
(:I C:-)	egg head/large brain
([(	Robocop
(8)	invisible man
(B ^ |	secret agent
(B-I=	modern art critic
(D)	welder
(-E:	bi-focals

(I	asleep
(V)=|	computer game champion
)	Cheshire Cat
) (	really separating
):-)	impish
)X->	devil
* :-0	alarmed!
*:-))	clown
*:**	fuzzy with a fuzzy moustache
*|	beautiful sunset
*|-0	still working at 5 a.m.
*8((:	strange
,':-C	huh? what's the matter? what's wrong?
,':-)	that's a really interesting idea!
...---...	S.O.S.
.V	duck
.-]	one-eyed
/:-)	salute
∧	camping and backpacking
: *	kisses
:- C	so shocked that jaw has hit the ground
:%)%	acne
:()	can't stop talking
:-(<|	standing firm
:-)—	skinny weakling
:-)(-:	just married!
:-)~(-:	lovers doing French kissing

:-)-0	smiling doctor with stethoscope
:*)	clowning
:/\)	extremely large nose
:/7)	Cyrano de Bergerac
:?)	philosopher
:[	really down
:-[	biting criticism
:-\	undecided
:-]	fake smile
:^(	nose put out of joint
:^D	great! I like it!
:-{	extra sad/about to cry
:-{}	blowing a kiss
:-|:-|	déjà vu
:-}X	wearing a bow-tie
:-~(	with bad cold
:-"	whistling
:-+	too much lipstick
:+(	punched nose, hurt
:+)	broken nose set
:-<	really sad
:-<	walrus
:<)	upturned nose
:<|	snooty
:->	bitingly sarcastic
:-6	exhausted/wipe out
:-a	touching tongue to nose

:-E]	needs to go to the dentist
:-F]	just came back from the dentist
:-i	half-smile
:-I	indifferent
:-M	speak no evil
:0	shocked
:-0	gobsmacked/disbelieving
:-o	wow!
:-0=	showing tongue to the doctor
:-0>-o	American tourist (note big mouth and camera)
:ol	with cold
:-P	sticking out tongue
:Q :@	what?
:-s	bizarre comment
:-S	confused; incoherent
:-t	cross
:-T	keeping a straight face
:-V	shouting
:-W	speaking with forked tongue
:-X	big wet kiss!
:-X	my lips are sealed; sworn to secrecy
:X)	hear no evil
:-Y	quiet aside
;-(...	crying lots
;-?	wry tongue in cheek
;-}	leering

;->	devilish wink
;>)	smirking
@-)	hypnotist
@@@@@@@:)	
	Marge Simpson
@}>-'-,—	rose
@-D	psychologist
[?	moving toward you and wondering about you?
[ ]	wanting to hug
[]	hug
_/	my glass is empty
\~/	full glass; my glass is full
\-o	bored
]?	moving away and wondering about you?
] [	separating
^	thumbs up
^(^	happy
^)^ ^(^	two people talking
{}	no comment
|^o 3-0	snoring
||*(	handshake offered
||*)	handshake accepted
}{	face-to-face (profile)
~~8}	snake
'-)	winking
+-(	shot between the eyes

<:-(:-e	disappointed
<:|-|)<	student of physics
<:-I	dunce
<:-0	Eeek!
<3	heart/love
-=#:-)	wizard
=):-)	Uncle Sam
=[0-)]	racing driver
=|:-)	Abraham Lincoln
=|:-)	top hat
=|:-) ~D	Englishman (with cup of tea)
=|:-)X	diplomat
> :-(	mad
>:-<	absolutely livid!
8	infinity
8-]	wow, maaan!
8^ | :-|	grim
8-|	eyes wide with surprise/in suspense
8->	just happy
8-0	Omigod!
8-0 —*	just before doubling over with pain
0 :-)	angelic/acting very innocent
X-(	dead

Michael O'Mara Books Limited

Now you can order other text-messaging books
directly from Michael O'Mara Books.

All at £1.99 each including postage (UK only)

HUMOUR

WAN2TLK? ltle bk of txt msgs – ISBN 1-85479-678-X
IH8U: ltle bk of txt abuse – ISBN 1-85479-832-4
LUVTLK: ltle bk of luv txt – ISBN 1-85479-890-1
RUUP4IT? ltle bk of txt d8s – ISBN 1-85479-892-8
URGr8! ltle bk of pwr txt – ISBN 1-8579-817-0
ltle bk of pics & tones – ISBN 1-8579-563-5

CHILDREN'S

The Wicked Book of txt jox – ISBN 1-903840-13-9
The Wicked Book of txt tlk – ISBN 1-903840-12-0

Postage and packing outside the UK:
Europe: add 20% of retail price
Rest of the world: add 30% of retail price

To order any Michael O'Mara book
please call our credit-card hotline: **020 8324 5652**

**Michael O'Mara Bookshop,
BVCD, 32–34 Park Royal Road, London NW10 7LN**